ACCESS AND BENEFIT SHARING: POLICY AND LEGAL IMPLICATIONS FOR PAPUA NEW GUINEA

EDITORS

Eric L Kwa
Sakarepe Kamene
John Kouni

UPNG Press and Bookshop
P. O. Box 413
University Post Office
National Capital District 134
Papua New Guinea

First published 2011

ISBN: 978-9980-84-897-0

Copies available with:

The Editors
C/-Associate Professor Eric L. Kwa
University of Papua New Guinea
School of Law
PO Box 317
University Post Office, NCD 134, Papua New Guinea
Fax: (675) 3267 187 *Tel:* (675) 3267 481
E-mail: ericlkwa@gmail.com

Dedication

This book is dedicated to Mrs Enaha Peri Kwa and Mr. Mark Opur, two young intellectuals of this country, who were called home by their Maker before the publication of the book.

Contributors

Associate Professor Eric L Kwa, PhD	*Senior Lecturer – UPNG Law School* PhD (Auckland), LLM (Hon) (Wollongong), LLB (Hon) (UPNG)
Professor Simon Saulei, PhD	*Director – Forest Research Institute* PhD (Aberdeen), MSc (Waterloo), BSc (Hon) (UPNG)
Dr. Alphonse Gelu	*Senior Research Fellow – National Research Institute* PhD (Auckland), MA, BA(Hon) UPNG
Mr. Sakerepe Kamene	*Lecturer – Linguistics Strand, UPNG School of Humanities and Social Science* MA (Monash), BEd, BA (Hon) (UPNG), Diploma (Teaching) (Goroka)
Mr. John Kouni	*Lecturer – UPNG Law School* LLM (IMLI, Malta), LLB (Waikato)
Ms. Enaha P Kwa	*Gender Advisor – Coffey International* MA (Politics) (UPNG), BA (Hon) (Wollongong)
Dr. Mange Matui	*Lecturer – UPNG Law School* LLM (London), LLB (Hon) (UPNG)
Mr. Mark Opur	*Senior Lawyer – Nonggorr Lawyers (Port Moresby)* LLM (Sydney), LLB (Hon) (UPNG)
Mr. Douveri Henao	*Trade Advisor – South Pacific Forum Secretariat* LLB (UPNG)
Mr. John-Mark G Genolagani	*Formerly Director – PINBio and currently Environmental Management and Development Specialist – DEC* Master EMD, (ANU), BSc (UPNG)

Table of Contents

Table of Statutes, Cases and Treaties

Statutes

Constitution
Conservation Areas Act 1978
Copyrights and Neighbouring Rights Act 2000
Customs Recognition Act (Cap 19)
Environment Act 2000
Environment (Permits) Regulation 2002
Environment (Prescribed Activities) Regulation 2002
Environment (Water Quality) Regulation 2002
Environment (Fees and Charges) Regulation 2002
Environment (Council's Procedure) Regulation 2002
Fauna (Protection and Control) Act
Fisheries Management Act 1998
Fisheries (Torres Strait Protected Zone) Act
Forestry Act 1991
Income Tax Act 1959
Income Tax (International Agreements) Act 1987
International Trade (Flora and Fauna) Control (Amendment) Act 2003
Land Act 1996
Lands Acquisition (Development Purposes) Act (Ch 9)
Local-level Governments Administration Act 1997
Mining Act 1992
National Agriculture and Research Institute Act 1996
National Parks Act 1982
National Parks Regulation
National Seas Act
Oil and Gas Act 1998
Organic Law on Provincial Governments and Local Level Governments 1995
Patents and Industrial Designs Act 2000
Patents and Industrial Designs Regulation 2002
Provincial Governments Administration Act 1997
Trade Marks Act
Stamp Duties Act

Cases

Supreme Court Reference Case No.7 1992 [1992] PNGLR 514
Ene Land Group Inc., -v- Fonsen Logging (PNG) Ltd and Another [1998] PNGLR 1

Forestry Act 1991 and the East New Britain Forestry Operations Control Act 1992
Vincent Ulelio and Others v Nelulu Land Group and Others [1998] PNGLR 31

Treaties

Agreement on Trade Related Aspects of Intellectual Property Rights
Convention on Biological Diversity
Convention on International Trade in Endangered Wild Species of Fauna and Flora
International Treaty on Plant Genetic Resources for Food and Agriculture
United Nations Convention on the Law of the Sea
World Heritage Convention

Abbreviations

ABS	Access and Benefit Sharing
CBD	Convention on Biological Diversity
CITES	Convention on International Trade in Wild Species of Fauna and Flora
CPC	Constitutional Planning Committee
DEC	Department of Environment and Conservation
FAO	Food and Agriculture Organization
FMA	Forest Management Agreement
GEF	Global Environment Facility
IMO	International Maritime Organization
INBio	Institute of Biodiversity
IPR	Intellectual Property Rights
ISO	International Standards Organization
ITPGRFA	International Treaty on Plant Genetic Resources for Food and Agriculture
LMA	Logging and Marketing Agreement
MPA	Marine Protected Area
MSR	Marine Scientific Research
MTA	Material Transfer Agreement
MTDS	Medium Term Development Strategy
NARI	National Agriculture and Research Institute
NFA	National Fisheries Authority
NGDP	National Goals and Directive Principles
OLPGLLG	Organic Law on Provincial Governments and Local-level Governments
PBA	Papua New Guinea Biodiversity Authority
PBR	Plant Breeder's Rights
PGRFA	Plant Genetic Resources for Food and Agriculture
PIC	Prior Informed Consent
PINBio	Papua New Guinea Institute of Biodiversity
R&D	Research and Development
SMTA	Standard Material Transfer Agreement
SPS	Sanitary and phytosanitary
TBT	Technical Barriers to Trade
TK	Traditional Knowledge
TRIPS	Agreement on Trade Related Aspects of Intellectual Property Rights
UNCLOS	United Nations Convention on the Law of the Sea
UNESCO	United Nations Educational Scientific and Cultural Organization
UNEP	United Nations Environment Program
WIPO	World Intellectual Property Organization
WMA	Wildlife Management Area
WTO	World Trade Organization

Acknowledgement

This book was made possible with the generous funding grant of the Department of Environment and Conservation and the Papua New Guinea Institute of Biodiversity. A special thanks to both organizations. We also thank Dr Wari Iamo (Chairman – Papua New Guinea Institute of Biodiversity and Professor Lohi Matainaho (Chairman – Technical Working Committee of the Papua New Guinea Institute of Biodiversity), for their support and involvement in this publication. The authors who have contributed papers to this book must be commended for their effort as for the first time in the country a book on environmental and biodiversity law has now been published.

Before the publication of this book, two contributors were called to be with their maker: Enaha Kwa and Mark Opur. We pay special tribute to them for their intellect, friendship and companionship. Their memories will forever linger in our hearts.

Ms Lois Stanley was responsible for typesetting. We acknowledge her support. We also thank the UPNG Press for publishing this book. Thank you to Dr John Evans and Mr Camillus Narokobi for their support.

Editors
2010

Foreword

This publication is a landmark initiative on genetic resources by the Government and marks the consolidation of various international, regional and national documentation to make it a reality in terms of the development of an appropriate policy and legal framework. This effort has been spearheaded by the Papua New Guinea Institute of Biodiversity (PINBio) in support of some core policy commitments and initiatives relating to biodiversity conservation, sustainable use of biodiversity and providing meaningful outcomes on access and benefit-sharing arrangements from the use of PNG's genetic resources by the Government through the Department of Environment and Conservation (DEC). While this continuing process has been funded by the Government's Public Investment Program (PIP) since 2001, much valuable funding support has also been provided by a number of non-governmental organizations including the World Wide Fund for Nature South Pacific Programme (WWF-SP) and Conservation International.

This publication is a result of the PINBio commissioning a report in 2004 and engaging Dr Eric Kwa from the University of Papua New Guinea (UPNG) while a doctoral scholar at Auckland University, New Zealand, on biodiversity law and policy in Papua New Guinea. This report was recently reviewed by a number of reviewers in Papua New Guinea (PNG) and that together with their own contributions, have formed the materials for this publication. The reviewers were: Dr Eric Kwa, Associate Professor at UPNG School of Law, Professor Simon Saulei, Director of the Forest Research Institute, Dr Alphonse Gelu, Senior Research Fellow at the National Research Institute, Mr Sakerepe Kamene, lecturer in the Linguistics Strand at the UPNG School of Humanities and Social Science, Mr John Kouni, lecturer in the Law Strand at the UPNG School of Law, Ms Enaha P. Kwa, Gender Advisor with Coffey International, Dr Mange Matui, lecturer in the Law Strand in the UPNG School of Law, Mr Mark Opur, senior lawyer with Nonggorr Lawyers in Port Moresby, and Mr Douveri Henao, Trade Advisor with the South Pacific Forum Secretariat.

I'm also pleased that a number of DEC officers have been involved over the years on the development of various reports in their respective roles, which have culminated in this publication. These officers include Mr Barnabas Wilmott and Mr Veari Kula from DEC's Wildlife Enforcement Branch, Dr Navu Kwapena and Mr Vagi Genorupa as head of the PINBio secretariat, Mr James Sabi as the Principal Ecologist in the Biodiversity Branch, Ms Yvonne Tio who was the head of the PINBio Secretariat, Dr Gae Gowae, the former Deputy Secretary of the Department (Conservation Division), and

John-Mark G Genolagani, the former First Assistant Secretary of the Conservation Division, who has been the driving force in this initiative.

I commend the valuable information and knowledge that will be imparted through this publication by PNG's own learned reviewers and other resource persons for their contributions. I am confident that this publication will set in train other developments for PNG communities to appreciate and take an active part in the advancement of a policy and law relating to fair and equitable sharing of benefits that arise from the use of genetic resources in PNG.

On behalf of PINBio and DEC I acknowledge the contributions by various experts and resource persons in this important undertaking.

Dr Warilea Iamo
Secretary for the Department of Environment and Conservation
Interim Chair for the Board of the Papua New Guinea Institute of Biodiversity

Chapter 1. Introduction

John-Mark G Genolagani and Eric Kwa

On 4 May 2006 there were two events that portray some contexts on the developments on environment policies in Papua New Guinea (PNG). The first is that it marked the occasion of the final sitting of the term of the National Parliament in session and set in motion the election for a new Government. There will be a reflection on how the Government has fared on the environmental front during the election period and optimism on the environmental agenda by the new Government. The second is a seemingly insignificant event - a stakeholders' consultation workshop to advance the maritime zoning undertaking under the auspices of the United Nations Convention on the Law of the Sea (UNCCLOS) by PNG.

This second event was being held in another wing of the national Parliament which did not raise the eyebrows of any public figures. A significant aspect of the maritime zones workshop was the issue of seabed mineral resources exploration being undertaken by Nautilus Minerals Niugini Ltd. This issue raised a wide array of questions, especially on the delineation of various jurisdictions in the sea. Although this was not the appropriate forum to discuss this specific issue, it was acknowledged by the group that the new Government will need to deliberate on this important issue because it may as well set a new environment agenda for the government.

Does the government have a mineral policy which is in tandem with environmental protection particularly in relation to oceans? Is the deep seabed mining exploration by Nautilus Minerals the catalyst to developing a holistic policy and legal framework on seabed mining and environment protection? These are critical issues that need to be addressed by the government. A law student from the University of Papua New Guinea (UPNG) participating in the workshop raised three pertinent points in a question, and these were:

- "What happens to the DNA being collected by Nautilus Minerals Niugini Ltd?;
- Is there going to be any technology transfer?; and
- What are the implications on intellectual property rights for PNG?"

These piercing points portray the relative short modern historical development by PNG of its biodiversity particularly access and benefit-sharing arrangements relating to the use of the country's genetic resources.

From the introduction on genetics and evolution, and biochemistry offered by the national universities, the subject matters on genetics and their development have been within the confined quarters of research scientists in such fields as agriculture, human health and pharmaceuticals, and universities. The turn of events in the 1980s and 1990s on the Hagahai Case that involved scientists from the PNG Institute of Medical Research brought PNG into the international limelight. In 1989 the Hagahai gene (human cell lines) were transferred to USA and the following year in 1990 the application to the US Patents and Trademarks Office was made. On 14 March 1995 the patent was issued. The US Patent 5,397,696 for a "Papua New Guinea human T-lymphotropic virus", was assigned to the Department of Health and Human Services. On 4 Oct 1995 the Rural Advancement Foundation International broke the news to the world and there was a massive public outcry especially by the international community. Given the sustained opposition to the patent, the USA National Institute of Health filed for the revocation of Patent 5,397,696 in October 1996 which was successful.[1]

As if the Hagahai case was only the tip of the ice-berg, another international scenario unfolded about the same time, which also brought PNG to the pinnacle of medical sciences and cultural intricacies. This time it was the global scare on the mad cow disease that was being linked to *kuru* in PNG in which the effects of cannibalism by the Fore people was of immense medical importance.[2] The interwoven nature of genes and medical research, genetic resources and a glimpse of PNG's socio-cultural settings are portrayed in another context. In her book review of Klitzman's memoirs on his experiences on the *kuru*, Richardson noted that, 'Everyone wants something. The Fore want money, the businessmen

---

[1] Kwa, E. L., "In the Wake of the Hagahai Patent: Policy and Legal Developments on Gene Ownership and Technology" in Mead, A and Ratuva, S (ed)., *Pacific Genes and Life Patents: Pacific Indigenous Experiences & Ownership of Life* (Wellington: COE/UNUIAS, 2007); Riodan, T, 1995. "Patents; A recent Patent on a Papua New Guinea Tribe's Cell Line Prompts Outrage and Charges of 'Biopiracy'". Accessed *The New York Times*, Wednesday, 27 May 2007; and Mooney, P and Hammond, E, *Re: Papua New Guinea Patents*, Rural Advancement Foundation International, Ottawa, Ontario, Canada, http//: www.charm.net/rafi~/rafi~home.html. Accessed 27 May, 2007.

[2] Richardson, S, "The Trembling Mountain: A Personal Memoir of Kuru, Cannibals, And Mad Cow Disease – a book review", at http://findarticles.com/p/articles/mi_m1511/is_v19/ai_20870327. Accessed 13 June, 2007.

want natural resources, the Christians want converts, and Klitzman wants medical history'.[3] She further reflects on Klitzman's advice on additional skills that physicians where physicians "should think like anthropologists in understanding patients; take less for granted, accept less as given".[4]

Busse and Whimp in their introduction to the interests and issues at hand on intellectual property rights on biological and cultural property in PNG, outlined some of the outsiders' perspectives on the actual and potential values inherent in PNG's traditions and customs.[5] This set the platform for the consolidation of PNG's status on the interests and issues for the development of an appropriate policy and legal framework on intellectual property rights through a collection of papers, discussions and recommendations presented in a Workshop in 1997.

Over the last three years the Government through the Department of Environment and Conservation has facilitated PNG's participation in the global and regional undertakings on biosafety under the auspices of the Cartagena Protocol on Biosafety to the Convention on Biological Diversity (Cartagena Protocol on Biosafety, 2000). The significance of this intervention is the awareness to another layer of stakeholders outside the previous domain of research scientists in terms of research and development opportunities and enterprise developments, on genetic resources in PNG. The question by the student of law mentioned above is a manifestation of interests that are now being generated across different disciplines. There is however, still a huge challenge on the awareness and education for the public at large to address PNG's vested interests and issues such as biotechnology, modern biotechnology and intellectual property rights relating to genetic resources.

The above snapshot is almost a quantum leap from some of the early scientific experiences in PNG. A dimension to this context is provided by Diamond in the *Prologue* of his award winning publication, *Guns, Germs and Steel*[6], where in 1972 a Papua New Guinean, Yali, asked Diamond:

> Why is it that you white people developed so much cargo and brought it to New Guinea, but we black people had little cargo of our own?

---

[3] Ibid

[4] Ibid

[5] Whimp, K. and Busse, M. (eds)., *Protection of Intellectual, Biological and Cultural Property in Papua New Guinea*, (Asia Pacific Press, Australian National University and Conservation Melanesia Inc, Port Moresby, 2000).

[6] Diamond, J., *Guns, Germs and Steel: The Fates of Human Societies*, (W. W. Norton and Company, New York and London, 1999).

These disparities between the 'whites' and the 'blacks' still haunt much of the present day PNG mentality and attitudes, especially the politicians and bureaucrats who have to provide a balance between economic development and environmental management. One of these dilemmas is the distinction between the previous socio-economic development policy frameworks and the paradigm shift to sustainable development in PNG. The latter calls for the full integration of environmental considerations in the current national development planning framework by the government.

There is strong optimism by the Government to strengthen its commitments on environment with particular attention on biodiversity conservation and sustainable utilization. There are new opportunities which PNG needs to harness in order to realize the actual and potential benefits of its genetic resources. On the commencement of the UNEP-GEF National Biosafety Framework project, the Minister for Environment and Conservation, Honorable William Duma provided the policy vision on biosafety and biotechnology with a direct reference to the development of the country's genetic resources by stating that:

> PNG should not be considered as a national museum of biodiversity and operate under strict protective measures. Our own scientists must rise up now and compete in the cutting edge of molecular biology to exploit opportunities that the technology presents. It is my belief that only when we ourselves have developed biotechnologies that we will also recognize the pitfalls and address our biosafety measures.

While there is a body of valuable information at hand to advance the policy framework on intellectual property rights, and the final draft policy and legal instrument on biosafety and biotechnology pertaining to genetic resources, Papua New Guineans must actively participate in opportunities such as intellectual property rights regimes and biotechnological developments. These changes and developments on genetic resources in PNG are documented in this book as a platform to advance an appropriate policy and legal framework.

This publication, as a continued support by the Papua New Guinea Institute of Biodiversity (PINBio), is PNG's initial attempt to capture the current status of interests and understanding of the issues at hand on the genetic resources from the international, regional and national perspectives in a policy and legal framework. One of the underlying objectives is also for the Government of PNG to fulfill its commitment as required by the third objective of the CBD which is:

> ...the fair and equitable sharing of the benefits arising out from the utilization of genetic resources .....

This book is derived primarily from an earlier initiative by the Papua New Guinea Institute of Biodiversity (PINBio)), which also supported relevant reviews required by the UNEP-GEF NBF project. The development of thoughts, ideas and various views on the ABS has been challenging given the nature of PNG's socio-political and economic situation, and which warrant appropriate responses by the Government. The ABS process has involved different stakeholders and understandably varying, differing and conflicting expectations and goals. It has attempted to capture various aspects of ABS and proposes a framework which lays the foundation to address some of the national matters and includes poverty alleviation through biodiversity conservation efforts to achieve sustainable development.

The main chapters (2-9) in this book are reviews undertaken by different specialists who reviewed the 2004 PINBio publication over a period of nine months from 2006 to 2007. The main chapters in the book are introduced in this introductory chapter.

Chapter 2 introduces the book by outlining some of the pertinent deficiencies currently in PNG within the contexts of a new approach to the development of national policies and the entailed legal instruments. It establishes the rationale in defining the relevant contexts of policy making and implications on law making in terms of a national ABS framework. Some of these concepts include the distinction between customary law and common law, and varied value systems that are inherent within the given socio-cultural and economic settings. Without an understanding of these key concepts and prevailing issues, the chapter asserts that the development of an appropriate policy and legal framework would be difficult and therefore for the first time attempts to draw the direct relationships on biological and genetic sciences to policy and law.

Chapter 3 introduces the reader to the current arrangements on ABS from the international, regional and national commitments under the auspices of various international treaties with particular reference to the CBD and its Bonn Guidelines on ABS arrangements. It highlights the interests and issues under international law and for these to be conceptualized into PNG's development of policy and legal processes. A significant introduction for PNG here is on implications of biological and genetic resources in international trade and national commerce, and includes thinking on how to approach the issues relating to intellectual property rights. The chapter in particular identifies some of the main difficulties faced by PNG which are not addressed by the CBD.

The concepts adopted by the CBD pertaining to the ABS are introduced in Chapter 4. The important subject matter is on the need to make a clear distinction on benefit-sharing as to, what are the benefits and who are the beneficiaries, and the actual or potential volumes that can be expected. These are cast against the status of poverty in PNG and asks whether the ABS policy and legal arrangements can promote poverty alleviation. The current nature of benefit-sharing from major industries such as fisheries, forestry and mining are considered to provide some guidance in the development of an ABS policy and legal framework.

The major considerations that PNG must bear given the current socio-political and economic situation is articulated within the contexts of some of the major policy developments that pose implications for biodiversity in PNG. The significance of principles in the development of the mining sector policy is brought into contention in the biodiversity policy development as a measure to fill the gaps in the national development plan framework which is articulated by the Medium Term Development Strategy. Chapter 5 offers a paradigm shift in the current approach that the government has adopted in formulating, adopting and implementing national policies.

Chapter 6 basically reviews the nature of law making arrangements in PNG and identifies the existing laws relating to biodiversity. Some of the recent laws that have adopted the principles of ABS, particularly in the minerals and the hydrocarbon sectors are considered together with the Draft Biosafety and Biotechnology Policy and Bill and the Maritime Delimitations Zones Bill.

Chapter 7 discusses the modern requirements of ABS insofar as research and development is concerned. This is based on the recognition that, *natural products provide an extremely broad biochemical diversity, distinct from those that are found in synthetic or combinatorial chemical libraries currently available and they show an extreme range of activity.* This discussion sets out, firstly, the main principles for access and benefit-sharing from research and development activities, and secondly, the need for promoting a harmonized system between and among the stakeholders and partners such as the researchers and their institutions, collaborators, governments and biological and cultural resource owners.

Chapter 8 focuses on intellectual property rights (IPR) and how it relates to the ABS. The arrangements need to take into account, the sources of the biological and genetic resources, access and benefit-sharing arrangements as defined by the given international and national policies and laws, and more particularly the potential commercialization of the valuable aspects of biological resources. It identifies as to what stage in the ABS process, the matters on IPR should be negotiated. The current legal framework in PNG on IPR is provided. This is advanced by highlighting the issues on scientific knowledge and traditional knowledge and identifies forward on the CBD's requirements in Article 8(j) and Article 15. In these discussions the significance of, access and prior informed consent, and benefit-sharing via its entailed material transfer agreements are highlighted. The latter essentially setting out the parties, their obligations and definition of benefits whether they are monetary or non-monetary.

Chapter 9 is crucial in its discussions as benefits need to be equated as to who or what can taxed or not, and casting the ABS within the taxation regime in PNG with a focus on IPRs in the first instance. The considerations of payments such as, environmental damages, royalty payments, milestone payments, and rewards from protection such as patents and copyrights are distinguished in the current legal taxation regime. The conclusion is provided in Chapter 10. This Chapter contains a set of recommendations for an appropriate law and policy for PNG.

The interests and issues on ABS in PNG captured in this publication are envisioned to stir a whole array of socio-political and economic questions in PNG. Some of the major issues have been highlighted in the different subject matters in the respective chapters and there is also an expectation that other local and national issues will emerge that have not been manifested to date. However, with this publication it is essential for developments in the ABS to contribute in a positive way through an appropriate national policy and law to respond to Kwa's reminder:

> The government has to make a serious commitment to its people and the environment through the reformation of the natural resources sector to comply with the constitutional directive. Successive governments have paid lip service to the development of a coherent system that will adequately cover the management of the natural resources for the benefit of the present and future generations. The time to act is now and not tomorrow.[7]

[7] Kwa, E. L., "Introduction", in Kwa, E. L (ed)., *Natural Resources Law of Papua New Guinea*, (Law Book Co, Sydney, 2000), (pp.1-5).

Chapter 2. Some General Principles and Trends relating to Access and Benefit Sharing

Sakarepe Kamene

Introduction

Developing an ABS framework for a country is a difficult task. To design a new system, one has to go through available literature and other sources to identify some current and major trends in ideas and issues about biodiversity, especially about PNG and its neighboring countries and states in the South Pacific and the world at large to use as a guide to develop the ABS framework. With such knowledge or information a strong and robust framework on ABS can be designed.

Literature on biodiversity, in particular, about accessing local knowledge, resources, benefit-sharing mechanisms, necessary laws and appropriate systems is sketchy in PNG. However, there are some current general principles and trends on biodiversity upon which appropriate laws and systems can be framed to best reflect PNG's socio-cultural, biological and ecological conditions.

The intention of the government is very clear. An ABS framework has to be developed for PNG. Once that is clear it is important to import necessary details that could go into the document to strengthen, enhance and facilitate not only tangible but also practical outcome. It is of paramount importance to envisage an involving, progressive or flexible law or policy to meet and cater for complex ethno-cultural diversity in PNG. Though it is important to tailor the ABS framework to reflect the local socio-economic and biological milieu, it is important to maintain some international perspectives. This is in keeping with the current global trends, practices, conventions and systems to share benefits associated with the exploitation of biological and ecological recourses.

A common understanding and appreciation of biodiversity scenario at the global level could make things all the much easier to design a people friendly system that benefits humanity. And not just a system that focuses merely on profit making and turning out surplus for the few. A profit driven system could place greater pressure on the existing biological resources. If this happens the consequences could be catastrophic on our lone planet and its inhabitants in particular.

The attempt to develop an ABS law and policy gives policy-makers the opportunity to change the current trend for the better for humankind. This requires re-thinking, and more importantly, a move away from the capitalist based idea where it continues to encourage individual pursuit and interest in accumulating wealth for the few. As experience shows it is not designed to spread benefits and wealth to humanity.

It is apparent now that the current capitalist system is more materialistic. Hence, it comes with a great social and economic cost. With capitalism, opportunities could diminish thus, increasing social and economic misery for the masses. Under such a condition only a handful of people may enjoy benefits derived from exploiting biological, cultural, economic and intellectual resources. Much of such resources are at the hands of indigenous peoples in developing or underdeveloped countries. But much of it leaves their shores and there is very little they enjoy in return. This is a real tragedy in most Third world countries. And there is every sign the situation is not getting any better at all at the present time.

With such a glooming picture it is highly critical that certain stringent measures be introduced to curtail global disaster. This is where law and policy-makers are needed to provide specific and relevant advice on sustainable use and management of biological diversity. In order to do that with confidence, experts in this area, need to consult some important and relevant resource materials. Such materials will guide law and policy-makers develop necessary and effective mechanisms, processes, procedures, policies and laws to regulate and monitor biodiversity conservation and sustainable use in the country.

Conceptual Framework

ABS is a process that involves many different concepts. Knowledge of the underlying values of these concepts will help policy-makers and implementers of law and policy give real meaning to this idea of access and benefit sharing.

When developing the ABS law and policy it is important to examine and re-examine concepts or ideas employed and used in law today. There is general consensus that concepts such as 'property', 'ownership', 'right', etc, were developed over time. The word 'property', for example, refers to all kinds of things. It refers to *objects* or *things* or to *relationship between persons* and *things*. Also it goes beyond that to include *'owning'* or *'being owned'* or *'possession'*. In English law, *property* refers to *a right in something* or *to something*. And *to own something* is to *have an 'enforceable claim'*. This is just one example to illustrate the multiplicity nature and extension of the semantic range of a particular word. It is important to bear this in mind when attempts are made to employ and use concepts in developing the ABS framework.

Developing Concepts

As gleaned from literature at the end of the 12th Century, land, in particular, in most parts of Europe was conceived in *'feudal terms'* – that is, land was seen as *'indivisible thing'*. But the Romans saw the *'thing'* as *property,* which *can be divided for almost infinitely*. This illustrates different views and perceptions communities and people have about legal concepts or words. More importantly, how they see and apply in their own socio-political and cultural contexts. In this light PNG could do better by vouching for ingenuity and insight in customary law.

When developing, coining and adopting concepts, policy-makers must be sensitive, more importantly, be ready to change prevailing attitudes and behaviors in the country. For example, laws and conventions do exist to regulate and control the ownership of property. But the question is whether or not they work effectively in meeting the needs and demands of the people. If this does not happen, then there is a chance to develop a new and appropriate legal system based on socio-cultural and political setting that best caters for people's aspirations and desires in resource development.

As mentioned earlier, such concepts take years to develop, expand, and become accepted in countries other than western countries. PNG is no exception. In that she uses the British Common Law legal system. But the question is, does this system have all the answers for every conflict in the country? This may imply something. In that just adopting a system or culture from another place or culture may not necessarily be adequate. It may require much more than that. This could require internal conditions to change in order to accommodate new innovations in modern PNG. Again a mere change is not enough. However, a change that is carefully fused with the local value system could have a better chance of being effective.

As the search for new ideas emerges, Papua New Guineans can turn to their traditional cultures to learn something. For example, when considering the concept of 'copyright', Simet turns to the Tolai experience and identifies the various levels of knowledge, and shows the concepts that capture and reflect the Tolai socio-cultural reality. He shows about 12 such levels of knowledge system that allow for the safe-keep of Tolai knowledge.[8] Such knowledge could be useful and can assist us develop a suitable legal system for PNG.

---

[8] Wimp, K. & Busse, M (eds.)., *Protection of Intellectual Biological & Cultural Property in Papua New Guinea.* (Canberra: Asia Pacific Press, 2000)

Simet acknowledges that there are knowledge involving supernatural forces – *turangan*, then there are sets of secret knowledge – *pidik*, there are songs and new knowledge or dreams – *barawon*, there are artistic skills or qualities – *buai* and so on. His discussion provides a useful background and scope for understanding the local knowledge systems and their practices. Such categories provide greater insights into our understanding of the world-view and thought patterns of traditional communities in PNG.

This could increase our knowledge on the cognitive frame of the Melanesian people thereby helping us to design laws and policies that are relevant and more practical to majority of people in this country. This is an area that requires special attention when developing the ABS framework. There is a price to pay though, if policy-makers choose not to consider existing concepts and systems in traditional communities. In the past century or so 'Westerner contempt' of indigenous knowledge cost them invaluable scientific information, but now they are beginning to appreciate traditional knowledge.

Whimp and Busse show that concepts or words are poly-semantics – that is, they have many more meanings. And if desired, a meaning or two can be brought to fore as the prime meaning(s) to produce greater impact on human behavior. They also note the work of Carrier[9] about attitudes of anthropologists who worked in PNG. Carrier observed that anthropologists often paid little attention to traditional concepts – in particular, his comment on the concept like 'property'. In their work anthropologist took the idea of 'property' for granted, and therefore did not develop it further to reflect the relationships and the values embodied in the word itself. There is a suggestion that anthropologists may not have understood the values embodied in such words.[10] A trap one must not fall into when dealing with or formulating laws for PNG.

This is a real challenge, which should be borne in mind when dealing with new or existing concepts so that appropriate terms with their associations are used to produce a tangible and practical outcome for PNG and its people. For concept development, a number of options could be considered:

- take existing concepts and make them relevant and suitable for PNG; or
- coin new concepts and ideas to meet the need and demands in PNG; or
- employ and use concepts that already exist in PNG communities and add new meanings to cater for new conditions.

---

[9] Carrier, J., "Property and Social Relations in Melanesia" in C.M. Hann (ed.), *Property Relations: Reviewing the Anthropological Tradition* (Cambridge: Cambridge University Press, 1998) pp 85-103.

[10] Note 1, supra at 1.

There are, of course, conceptual issues. Take for example, Carrier's concepts of *'commodity economies'* and *'gift economies'*. Whimp and Busse observed the two ideas represented a marked contrast in the economic systems and activities in Melanesia and the Western world. Noting further that in Melanesia 'gift economy' signifies that 'property' is not totally alienated or given away as in Western societies where property is conceived as a commodity.[11] In that it can be bought and sold. And it is alienated completely from its initial owner. This does not happen in Melanesia. So any law that runs contrary to this perception in Melanesia could pose more problems for PNG.

In Melanesia, however, property is viewed, as a gift being exchanged for a particular reason or purpose. Often it is done to provide security, renew, maintain or mend relationship or alliance. Property is, therefore, never totally given away. It is there within their perceived and reachable relational realm, and more importantly, can be recalled at some later time. And to return, one often pays or meets necessary conditions to have the property returned to the original owner. This seems a normal way of transacting property in many Melanesian communities. This explanation is useful to understanding the notion of 'property', and its benefit-sharing arrangements in Melanesia. Such a concept could be used as the basis for designing the ABS law for PNG.

Another concept which is synonymous with Melanesian cultures is the notion of reciprocity. Muke provides not only interesting but also an important account and challenge by Ongka – the chief of the Kawelka people of the Western Highlands of PNG. According to Ongka – 'intellectual creativity' is like an investment for the future.[12] He compares this with a seed. If the seed is successful, and grows into a tree and bears fruit, then those who benefited from the fruit are indebted to the original source.

Considering Ongka's statement and the cultural principle of *'reciprocity'*, Ongka has a cultural base for issuing a courageous challenge to western scholars and others who exploit intellectual property of the local people. His challenge appears to suggest the future direction where scholars and others could be challenged and restricted in this area. The challenge needs to be taken seriously. And if possible, incorporate the ideas, practices and sentiments expressed here in the new law on ABS. This could be a pre-condition to produce the best and tangible outcome.

[11] Ibid, 17.
[12] Ibid, 96.

Common Law vs. Customary Law

This issue relates to the application of the common law to culturally different communities. At independence the *Constitution* adopted the spirit of custom and English common law as the country's 'underlying law'. The *Constitution* also recognizes that if custom is inconsistent with a statute or not repugnant to the principles of humanity, it can be adopted and applied as part of the underlying law.

The *Constitution* further provides legal conditions that where there is no statute law or customary law regarding a particular issue or problem then custom must take precedence over common law. This may sound all too easy. However, it does raise a fundamental question of one's 'ability' or 'competence' in interpreting, appropriating and applying customary law in a convincing way to amicably resolve issues arising from resource development. Any new legal framework must be responsive to such conditions. More work and debate may be required in this area.

Covert and condescending attitudes of PNG elites, especially the lawyers must change, if PNG is to improve its legal system to best reflect local socio-political and cultural conditions. But the quest for new ideas, systems or institutions is not all that too easy. Young, an ethnographer, while working among the Kalauna people of Goodenough Island, Milne Bay Province, observes and warns that introduced ideas, systems or institutions replace the existing local systems or institutions.[13] And when there is a local problem, the introduced system is not able to resolve the local problem - also the local institution or system is no longer there – one that is or was able to alleviate the local issue. The issue persists, disorientates and causes misery among Kaluna people. This experience could easily hold true for other communities in the country.

There is the question of 'what might be perceived as the best system or law' in culturally complex and pluralistic country like PNG remains a thorny point for policy and law-makers. This may pose an immediate challenge to law and policy makers. This is one area that may require greater focus and attention when developing a legal framework or policy-related matters in the country.

What kind of Biodiversity Legal Framework?

One best way of looking at this question is by considering the pluralistic nature of PNG. It is utmost critical at this point to examine the needs, demands, interests and characteristics of competing groups in relation to

[13] Young, M., *Fighting with Food: Leadership, Values and Social Control in a Masin Society* (Cambridge: Cambridge University Press, 1971).

resource development. This is where Filer's idea of *'social drama'* could be useful for policy and law-makers.

'Social Drama' – or 'Legal Drama' – 'Evolving Legal Framework'

The national vision of ABS framework should constitute what Filer calls *'social drama'*[14] or to make it relevant for our purpose – *'legal drama'*. Here 'legal drama' gives a more 'legal flavor or slant' to dealing with the issue or conflict than the social notion dealt with in Filer. It is, of course, a theatrical notion of having a variety of actors or participants acting in different scenes within the major theme or issue. Under such a situation everyone is given a chance or opportunity to play his or her role but within a given issue or theme, which could continue for sometime, and reveal the plot to the audience. In other words, everyone involved arrives at a general but common understanding that is satisfactory to all concerned in the issue.

In 'legal drama' there are various parties involved. They could be non-governmental organizations, resource owners, lawyers, law and policy-makers, developers, concerned citizens, affected communities, and so on. Each group or individual is playing its part to presenting the case or issue in order to reach an amicable resolution. The idea has the cultural base. It fits well with the consensus principle in Melanesia where every actor is given a chance to come to a 'common ground' in order to resolve a conflict. Greater understanding of such notions could help policy and law-makers to formulate relevant and more practical ABS law and policy.

There is yet another facet to this notion of legal drama. In that such a system should entail an evolving legal framework. That is, it is flexible enough, and can adequately cater for everyone's interests and desires at any point in time in resource development. In particular, the issues and conflicts that arise from exploiting ecological and biodiversity resources. Furthermore, such a legal system must remain vibrant and elastic in its character. That is it must have the ability to expand, contract and extend beyond the limit to embrace the needs and desires of various competing parties.

Filer argues that policies or laws, for that matter, should not be left at the hands of technical people or elites. He argues for more involvement of other interested parties and stakeholders in the process of developing any public document. In this way the public at large is given some sense of involvement and participation in making the document. He further notes that where stakeholders are not part, the technocrats often come up with fancy and technical documents that fail to serve the purpose for which it is intended.

---

[14] See Filer, C., *Loggers, Donors, Resource Owners* (London: International Institute for Environment and Development & National Research Institute, 1998).

Any legal framework on ABS should be unique. It must be something special that PNG must offer to the world at large in this area. It should entail and reflect local socio-cultural contexts, and therefore, should not be heavily dependent on external legal forces or factors. Even though external legal framework may remain an important consideration, it may be taken only as a guiding principle to design our own legal regime.

PINBio Report of 2004[15]

In 2004, PINBio initiated the first project on ABS. The work was undertaken by Dr. Kwa who submitted a report commonly called the 'Kwa Report' or 'document'. The Report provides comprehensive details of current conventions, acts, procedures, institutions, etc, that in one way or other deal with specific areas in biodiversity. It lists both external and internal conventions, legislation, etc, that govern or regulate ecological and biodiversity resources and other related areas. Some invaluable lessons and information are drawn from the Kwa Report for this text.

The most important aspect of the Kwa document involves the recommendations. In particular, *Recommendation One*, which appears attractive. This recommendation is a good one. But it may require further work to enable the government to establish a Papua New Guinea Biodiversity Authority or a similar institution which could perform the powers and functions as envisioned. The idea is well worth developing into a tangible infrastructural outlay with coordination as its central function.

Kwa's work has invaluable information, showing some general and specific laws and acts on biodiversity and related-areas or specific topics, issues and challenges in the country. His work on 'Biodiversity Law and Policy in Papua New Guinea,' appears to be something of an innovation, and is very useful for developing the ABS framework. Studies of this sort provide new and up-to-date data on biodiversity help in developing a specific legal framework for PNG and its people.

Intrinsic Biological Values

Sekhran and Miller observe that PNG does not only have a complex but also a rich ecosystem with considerable biological diversity with an 'intrinsic value'.[16] This means that other species enjoy deriving benefits from existence of others. Loss of other species could endanger the intricate balance of the ecosystem, which could eventually result in severe social,

---

[15] Papua New Institute of Biodiversity., *Biodiversity Law and Policy in Papua New Guinea* (Port Moresby: PINBio, 2004). Also loosely referred to as the "Kwa Report" or document.

[16] Sekhran, N & Miller, S (eds.)., *Papua New Guinea Country Study on Biological Diversity* (Port Moresby: Department of Environment & Conservation, Conservation Resource Centre & the African Centre for Resources & Environment (ACRE), 1995).

economic and ecological deprivation causing irreparable and irreversible damage to fragile ecological system. This could be catastrophic. And every effort must be made at all cost to prevent it.

Today Papua New Guineans may accrue and enjoy real economic benefits, but the cost would be high for future generations. This is a sentiment worth keeping in mind when it comes to developing new policies and laws on resource development. It could be a useful guide in shaping better outcomes for the future generation.

There is also an economic reason for biodiversity conservation and sustainable use in PNG. Biodiversity obviously has the nation's '*primary resource-based economy'*, which supports and protects social and economic systems. Over exploitation of biological diversity without due care to its importance in sustaining other forms of life could have catastrophic impact on other species. For this and other reasons Sekhran and Miller strongly recommend conservation and prudent management as measures to protect biological diversity.[17]

Natural Capital vs. Capitalism

New approaches, innovations and techniques are needed in developing biological diversity and ecological resources in a more manageable and sustainable way to alleviate pressures on the fragile ecosystem. The current unscrupulous economic system is out there to make more money, and is less concerned about the safety of the ecosystem.

Over exploitation of PNG's ecological resources is already showing signs of environmental fatigue. This is already threatening the fragile ecological system. If this trend continues, and goes beyond the renewable capacity coupled with abuse caused by dumping of waste, the country could be in for more trouble than what the present generation bargained for in the first place. The situation demands immediate affirmative actions to alleviate ecological disaster. This requires a new and innovative model to address the issue.

This is where Sekhran and Miller's idea of 'natural capital' becomes an important consideration. Natural capital is an interesting idea. In that it takes a broader view of production factors by considering or incorporating 'stocks of ecological assets' and its natural production function embedded within the system itself. More importantly, the system has some fundamental principles, processes and elements with each one having its own internal structure that has taken many years to develop and mature. Because of this, all the delicate parts must work together to sustain the delicate ecological balance. Any disturbance could threaten the fragile ecosystem. If this happens its consequence to humanity could be fatal to humanity. This

---

[17] Ibid, 13.

certainly demands immediate affirmative action to eliminate or minimize risks in the future.

Proper analysis will show that from natural capital, service flows into the economic system. The system maintains ecological balance. This, in turn, shapes or makes a contribution to final products. Natural system involves complex processes combined with conventional production factors completing the general picture of what comes out as final product. Contributions by natural system to shape final product is not always visible, making it difficult to visualize how delicate the system is. Hence, it obfuscates people's perception of the system. With misguided perception, people tend to over exploit and abuse the environment. This is a danger that needs immediate attention from concerned people. In this case appropriate laws, mechanisms, procedures, institutions and policies may be needed immediately to address such issues. In this respect an ABS framework is not only timely but a worthwhile effort for PNG.

It is noteworthy that many services provided by natural capital subsidize economic activities – for example – the sink function in reducing the cost of waste disposal. Also it helps in maintaining the health, and further promoting the productivity of labor. Many of the benefits are hidden and are not often obvious to humankind. This makes it extremely difficult to convince people to promote sustainable way of dealing with our fragile ecological resources. Natural capital appears better suited to traditional conditions where traditional people are closely linked and dependent on nature for supply and services – not human and man-made supply- as notable in western societies.

At this juncture there is a need to say a few things about natural capital as opposed to capitalism – the current economic system. Capitalism is the dominant economic idea at present. And it is seen and felt as the main offender in creating demands for overexploitation of natural resources. It allows fewer people to accumulate wealth at the expense of majority of resource owners, mostly in poor or developing countries, and often creates conditions of irreversible poverty. It is less cultural, but more materialistic in its tendency. Also it is not concerned with humanity. It is driven by high economic gains and excessive surplus. Under such a system – capitalism – exerts high human and environmental cost. If this continues at the current pace and trend it could pose an immediate and eminent danger to the ecosystem. We may pay a hefty price for upsetting the intricate ecological balance. Every effort must be made to retain its natural state so humanity can continue to enjoy its varied and not so obvious benefits the system offers.

Natural capital, on the other hand, brings to fore the value of men and its connection to environment. A more spiritualized connection to using ecological resources, allowing a more sustainable and prudent ecological and environmental management system to come into play. Also it keeps the natural balance thereby enhancing the vibrant ecological system for the betterment of humanity. This could be the way forward for our future generations.

Spiritualization of Environment

The concept of cosmology and the environment in PNG is well presented by Paschal Waisi.[18] When describing the world-view of the Laufis of the Sadaun Province, he notes the Laufis' intimate connection with *Kuplongo* – a local supernatural deity. *Kuplongo* possesses supernatural powers upon which all human fate and activities depend. And the Laufis think that their well-being is highly dependent on their ability to communicate with *Kuplongo* – the supernatural being.

Kuplongo manifests itself through four other spirits – the *mangers* – the good spirits, the *tanofos* – the bad spirits, the *toas* – the evil spirits – they threaten people's lives, and the *ririm* – a combination of good and bad spirits – they are harmless and bring comfort, peace and harmony to people. Waisi's discussion shows a process of spiritualization of the environment. What is more, the process continues to sanctify one's surroundings thus, providing sound moral and management basis for the sustainable use of their ecological resources.

Waisi's study can help policy and law-makers incorporate 'spirituality' as one of the local principles in formulating the ABS framework. More respect could be derived through incorporating local ideas and data. Such studies also give insights into thought patterns and processes of the indigene people. Greater understanding of the local conditions and reality could assist in designing suitable legal framework for our people.

Experience, over the years, also shows that complex laws that depend only on legal experts for their interpretation have remained costly and out of reach for ordinary people. More often than not such laws have become less effective and are of little use to the people. For this reason PNG needs to re-think along the lines of other developing nations, and not behave and employ complicated or highly sophisticated ideas or systems of the developed world, to design appropriate laws and policies that best reflect her own socio-political and economic conditions.

---

[18] Waise, P., *The Lau'um People: A Historical & Philosophical Analysis on their History and Traditions* (Port Moresby: UPNG Press, 2000).

On Bio-cultural Diversity: Linking Language, Knowledge and the Environment

Bio-cultural diversity is an important concept that must be considered in the development of the ABS framework. It covers a whole host of topics and issues. Topics such as coevolution of cultural, linguistics and biological diversity, the value of ecological knowledge, threat to indigenous knowledge and cultural perception of ecological interactions are all embraced by this concept. All areas must be explored to find suitable principles for developing an ABS framework for PNG.

Other discussions highlight immediate consequences of losing local knowledge and information. Loss of certain local information or knowledge could be life threatening in particular communities. The point is well made by Harmon in Maffi where he notes 'diversity in peril' showing that humans are fast approaching a 'momentous threshold' – a point of no return, where a critical amount of both biological and cultural diversity could be lost forever and may never again be re-generated in any time scale significant to the development of humankind.[19] Loss of knowledge could make way for regression to emerge as a new social order. And regression could pose a barrier in our effort to initiate any new innovation. This could isolate PNG and its people from fully participating in the ever-increasing demands of the global community. Under such a condition, poverty is likely to ensue and take hold of PNG. With this remains a real possibility, PNG needs an immediate affirmative action to arrest the country falling into such a tragic situation in the future.

Mishler notes the pressures of development are causing "an alarming increase in the rate of extinction in biodiversity." He points out that many will become extinct before societies even know them. This he notes as "a double tragedy".[20] Maffi calls for urgent action to save indigenous languages, knowledge and oral tradition.[21] More action is needed in these areas to re-vitalize and maintain such aspects of many indigenous peoples of the world. In this respect any law or policy proposed for local people must not replace or eliminate the existing knowledge or linguistic system, but that they be strengthened through the regulatory framework.

Summary

Designing an ABS without understanding some of the key concepts and issues from a cultural perspective is like a ship out in the raging sea without

---

[19] Lusia, M (ed.)., *On Biocultural Diversity: Linking Language, Knowledge, and the Environment* (Washington: Smithsonian Institution Press, 1998) 6.
[20] Ibid, 71.
[21] Ibid, 413-432.

a compass to find the way home. The issues raised also highlight the range and depth that the ABS framework should be applied.

The ABS framework must be both holistic and flexible to enable the coverage and accommodation of the changing patterns in human behaviour. The message in this Chapter is clear – the content and context of the ABS framework must be influenced by traditional values and principles which form the lifeline of the majority of the people in the country.

Chapter 3. Access and Benefit Sharing and International Law

Douveri Henao

Introduction

The use of knowledge to change, modify or harness the biological resources for the benefit of humans is as old as the story of Adam and Eve in the Garden of Eden. Throughout the course of history, people have gained various types of skills, knowledge and experiences relating to various aspects of the environment and natural resources to improve their livelihood.

Over the years attempts have been made at the international level to access this pool of biological knowledge and skills to enable the equitable sharing and utilization of these knowledge and skills to improve the living conditions of humans on a global scale. But accessing these biological knowledge and skills also requires appropriate safeguards to protect the interests of the holders of these knowledge and skills and also to compensate them through transparent and simple schemes.

The search for an appropriate mechanism to enable the access to sustainable use of genetic resources and biological knowledge and skills, and the equitable sharing of benefits arising from the use of these knowledge and skills culminated in the formulation and adoption of the Convention on Biological Diversity (CBD) in 1992. The CBD therefore provides the basic framework for access to and sustainable use of genetic resources, use and sharing of biological knowledge and skills and the conservation of biological diversity. The key provisions of the CBD which are relevant for present purposes are: Articles 2, 8j, 12.4, and 15-20. These provisions will be considered throughout this Chapter.

Some Conceptual Issues

There are several conceptual issues that require some clarification to enable the reader to have a better understanding of the issues at hand. These conceptual issues are: (1) ABS; (2) biological diversity; (3) access; and (4) benefit sharing.

Access and Benefit Sharing

At the outset, it is imperative to consider the definition of ABS. What ABS? A clear and appropriate definition of this concept is imperative. Unfortunately, there is no legal definition of ABS in the CBD or any other international treaty. At the international level, some attempts have been made to provide some general guidelines relating to ABS. Some of these guidelines are descriptive while others are prescriptive. Descriptive principles are usually procedural in nature and operate as a guide. Prescriptive rules on the other hand are substantive and must be seen to be implemented.

An example of a descriptive principle relating to ABS is Article 8j of the CBD. The provision merely states that where traditional knowledge (TK) is utilized for the development of genetic resources, the holders of the TK must share in the benefits arising from the use of that TK. Whereby benefit sharing must be given when traditional knowledge is utilized for innovation and practices. An example of a prescriptive rule can be seen in the form of a standard Material Transfer Agreement (sMTA) under Article 12.4 of the International Treaty on Plant Genetic Resources for Food and Agriculture (ITPGRFA). This provision clearly states that where a standard Material Transfer Agreement has been adopted it cannot be modified or amended.

Biodiversity

The second concept that requires clarification is biological diversity. Article 2 of the CBD defines biodiversity as:

> Means the variability among living organisms from all resources including *inter alia,* terrestrial, marine and other aquatic ecosystems and the ecological complexes of which they are part; this includes diversity within species, between species and of ecosystems.

Biodiversity therefore consists of living organisms located in terrestrial and marine and other aquatic ecosystems. The definition embraces *diversity between species* and *within species*. The CBD definition of biodiversity is holistic and requires a holistic approach for the utilization and management of biological diversity.

Access

The third concept – access – in simple terms means 'allowing' or 'permitting' the use of something. 'Access to' connotes a relationship between two or more parties. On the one hand is the party that requires access, and on the other hand, is the party that must allow or permit access. In relation to genetic resources, the first party requires access to genetic resources while the second party who is the possessor or owner of the genetic resource must give permission to the first party to obtain the genetic resources.

The relevant provision of the CBD that deals with access is Article 15. The provision declares that States have sovereign rights over their natural resources as well as the genetic resources and access to these resources must be determined by the States through national legislation. The rules of access adopted by the State should however not be difficult so as to negate access.

Article 15(3) provides that where genetic materials which were accessed by a party are utilized through the use of biotechnology, the country of origin must be properly acknowledged. And Article 15(4) states that to compliment national legislation, mutually agreed terms can be established in an agreement to facilitate access. At the center of such mutually agreed terms is *prior informed consent* (PIC) which must usually be sought from the provider. Under Article 15(6), recipients of access must endeavor to collaborate with the provider country's scientists in research and development (R&D) activities relating to genetic material.

Benefit Sharing

The critical provision relating to benefit sharing is Article 15(7). The provision reads:

> Each Contracting Party shall take legislative, administrative or policy measures, as appropriate, and in accordance with Article 16 and 19 and, where necessary, through the financial mechanisms established by Article 20 and 21 with the aim of sharing in a fair and equitable way the results of research and development and the benefits arising from the commercial and other utilization of genetic resources with the Contracting Party providing such resources. Such sharing shall be upon mutually agreed terms.

This provision requires that benefit sharing arrangements between the recipient and provider of genetic material based on mutually agreed terms must embrace technology transfer principles in Article 16 as well as benefits derived from biotechnology as provided under Article 19. Monetary benefits must also be incorporated in the ABS arrangement as required under Articles 20 and 21.

The general rule is that the benefits must be shared on a *fair and equitable* basis. The terms of a benefit sharing agreement must be mutually agreed upon by the relevant parties. The challenge is to design an appropriate modality for benefit sharing. Benefits can either be in monetary (Articles 20 and 21) or non-monetary form (Articles 16 - 19) or a combination of both.

Articles 20 and 21 provide for monetary benefits. These Articles provide the framework for access and utilization of financial resources in the development of genetic resources to assist and encourage developing and least developing countries implement the Convention.

There are three forms of monetary benefits. These consist of access fees, one off compensation payment and licensing rights over patents.

- access of the genetic material – access fees;
- access to TK - one off compensation payment for the use of the knowledge or alternatively co-patent or licence holder; and
- access to scientific knowledge (and collaboration) - one off compensation payment for the use of the knowledge or alternatively co-patent or licence holder.

Access fees are based on the user pay principle. In other words, the provider will put a fee and the recipient is to pay. Whereas the one off compensation and licensing rights relates to two different legal aspects of intellectual property. First, the compensation payment effectively means the provider of the TK or the scientific knowledge wants just compensation of the knowledge rendered and has no intention of perpetuating the ownership of the process or product. Second, the licensing arrangement identifies co-ownership of the patent and therefore co-sharing of the benefits from the commercialization of the process or product. This would mean that as long as the patent is applicable, the monetary benefits derived from its commercialization will be shared with the TK owner or the scientist.

The non-monetary benefits of access to and use of genetic resources are provided under Articles 16, 17, 18 and 19. Article 16 relates to technology transfer. This includes transfer of biotechnology techniques or processes that are not harmful to the environment (Article 15(1)). The transfer of technology can be to a private as well as government institutions. Where the technology transfer also involves intellectual property rights (IPR), access to the technology will be subject to the terms and conditions of the registered IPR.

Article 17 covers exchange of information. The information which is the subject of exchange can be:

- technical;
- scientific;
- socio-economic research;
- training and surveying programmes;
- specialized knowledge;
- indigenous and traditional knowledge; and
- biotechnology.

Article 18 promotes collaboration between stakeholders who are involved in biodiversity research. The research collaboration must promote institutional strengthening and human capacity building. This cooperation must be governed by national legislation or polices. Key objectives of the legislation or policy must be: (1) development of technologies, including TK technologies; (2) training of personal; and (3) exchange of experts. Where there are no legal or policy frameworks, the collaboration can be governed by an agreement. However, where a national policy or legislation exists, a mutual agreement can also be adopted to strengthen the arrangement.

Benefits arising from the use of biotechnology and the sharing of those benefits are governed by Article 19. Article 19(2) reads:

> Each Contracting Party shall take all practicable measures to promote and advance priority access on a fair and equitable basis by Contracting Parties, especially developing countries, to the results and benefits arising from biotechnologies based upon genetic resources provided by those Contracting Parties. Such access shall be on mutually agreed terms.

This Article should be read in tandem with the Cartagena Protocol on Biosafety. Basically, the provision encourages the active involvement of nationals from developing countries in biotechnological research and development.

The formulation of an appropriate regulatory framework that promotes fair and just sharing of benefits arising from the access and use of genetic resources is imperative.

ABS in Other Relevant Treaties

There are three other significant treaties that have a bearing on ABS. These are: (1) United Nations Convention on the Law of the Sea (UNCLOS); (2) ITPGRFA; and (3) Agreement on Trade Related Aspects of Intellectual Property Rights (TRIPS). It is essential to consider the provisions of these international agreements as they relate to ABS because they have important bearings on national ABS regulatory frameworks.

Access and Benefit Sharing and UNCLOS

The UNCLOS is the international treaty relating to the sea and its natural resources. The treaty was concluded in 1982. The treaty among other things, promotes peaceful uses of the seas and oceans, the equitable and efficient utilization of their resources, the protection and conservation of the marine living resources, the study and particularly the marine scientific research of the marine environment.

ABS relating to the use of marine genetic materials and resources is embraced by Part XIII (Articles 238-265) of the treaty which relates to marine scientific research. Article 246(5) of UNCLOS which is similar to Article 15(1) of the CBD, empowers coastal States to exercise their discretion to either deny or allow access for marine scientific research, even if the research is of direct benefit to the State. Where access is granted the provision states that States may require a prior agreement to be executed containing additional conditions before a research is conducted. This requirement is indeed similar to Article 15 (5) of the CBD which provides that PIC must be sought from the provider before access is allowed.

Some of the benefits that can be derived from marine scientific research relating to marine genetic materials are shown in Table 1.

Table 1: *Monetary and Non-monetary Benefits from MSR*

Non Monetary Benefits	**Monetary Benefits**
-joint research in Papua New Guinea to increase scientific capacity -training of local scientists in laboratories of research countries in terms of fellowships, work attachments or long term exchange of research programs between PNG and Research Country/competent international organization, during research trials, or during product discovery and development or during drug trials. Special agreements may be made in this regard. -identification of national institution to monitor processes involved -communication of results to national or provincial scientific institutions -acknowledgement in publication -participation in planning and decision making - access to and control over samples and research results -specimens deposited in national institutions or seed banks -co-ownership of intellectual property rights, for instance joint licensing of patents -obligations of third parties licensees to share benefits with the national research institutions -technology transfer of equipment and material. Special agreements may be made to specify precise nature of technology transfer and equipment. -development of trade secrets -training in bio prospecting methods, collection and preparation of samples, bio diversity monitoring, socioeconomic monitoring, and other training as the need arises.	-Bio prospecting fees -sample fees -contribution to the research budget of the national research institution where long term exchange programs are in place between Papua New Guinea and Research Country. This may be set out in an agreement. -percentage of royalties be made to provincial grant fund for the benefit of the local communities in the maritime provinces where the resources are found -commitment to re-supply of samples to the Papua New Guinea institution -trust funds to be established for conservation programs in the maritime provinces. These may be subject of special agreements. -royalties generated from licenses of intellectual property rights may go to the benefit of on-going projects for research and bio diversity conservation.

Although, Part XIII of UNCLOS generally allows for access in the different maritime zones of a coastal States for MSR, subject to the principles, rights and obligations of the States in these areas, it is clear that certain aspects of the marine environment such as biodiversity and ecosystems of the marine environment have not been sufficiently dealt with by the Law of the Sea Convention. For instance, the marine scientific research provisions under Part XIII promote the exploitation of 'genetic resources' whereas the CBD calls for the conservation and sustainable use of genetic resources. Finding the synergy to ensure compatibility of these two treaties has been the challenge for the international community.

As a start Article 22 of the CBD has provided that critical link between the CBD and UNCLOS. This provision calls for the implementation of the Convention with respect to the marine environment consistently with the rights and obligations of States under the 1982 Law of the Sea Convention except where the exercise of those rights and obligations cause damage or threat to bio-diversity. In this respect, through the framework of the CBD, moves have been initiated since about 1997 to address the concerns of the Convention through a holistic ecosystemic approach. Hence, the recommendations to international organizations such as United Nations Environment Program, UNESCO, International Maritime Organization, Food and Agriculture Organization and the World Bank to take heed of this approach in their action plans thus, creating linkages with the various international conventions that call for similar or like actions.

With particular reference to marine and coastal bio-diversity it is observed that the scientific understanding of the marine environment is fundamental to the sound development of the marine resources, as well as to the protection and preservation of the marine environment as a whole. Through the framework of UNEP, Jakarta Mandate on Marine and Coastal Biological Diversity as adopted by the Conference of the Parties addresses the global consensus on the importance of marine and coastal biological diversity as part of implementation of the *Convention on Biological Diversity.* Many cross-cutting issues have been highlighted within the context of the Jakarta Mandate, one of which is '*Access to Genetic Resources and Benefit Sharing*'.

Recent Proposals

In an effort to develop a synergy between the CBD and the UNCLOS, the government has engaged the services of the Commonwealth Secretariat to assist PNG in developing its maritime zones legislation. The aim of the project is to assist PNG implement the provisions of the UNCLOS relating to maritime zones and their uses. One of the key proposals is to implement Article 194(1) of UNCLOS relating to the prevention, reduction and control of pollution of the marine environment. A draft Maritime Delimitation Zones Bill has now been formulated with the assistance of the Commonwealth Secretariat. Some of the key provisions of the Bill relate to:

- designation of the territorial sea, contiguous zone and exclusive economic zone;
- fishing reserves;
- marine protection areas;
- marine scientific research; and
- marine scientific research committee.

Measures to protect and conserve marine biological resources will be provided under the proposed law. Access to marine genetic resources will also be regulated by the new Bill.

Access and Benefit Sharing of plant genetic resources for food and agriculture under the ITPGRFA

Using the same concept of ABS in the CBD, (where the intention is to allow access to genetic material, traditional knowledge or scientific knowledge) the ITPGRFA specifies the genetic material for plant genetic resources for food and agriculture that can be accessed under Appendix 1. It then departs significantly from the CBD by advocating multilateral access to these plant genetic resources for food and agriculture (PGRFA). It also states that there should be no barriers of IPR. The main argument against IPR barriers is that these plant genetic resources for food and agriculture (which are technically genetic materials) are used by 80% of the world population and therefore are important for food security purposes.

Under any form of agreement, a certain party will have the legal subject, in this case the PGRFA, while another aspires to attain it. In this case, it is the provider that has the plant genetic resource and the recipient who is eager to have possession over it. The provider possesses the plant genetic resource IPR, discoveries and general conservation collections whether *ex situ* field collections, in vitro *in situ* collections or seedlings.

As mentioned above the ITPGRFA through Appendix 1 specifies which PGRFA that can be accessed. By specifying these plant genetic resources, the treaty allows multilateral access to these crops in contracting parties' gene banks. The party of course, in this case, is the country that has signed up to the treaty. It would seem that gene banks in a particular country are now subject to the ITPGRFA as well as the sMTA.

A key element of ITPGRFA is that it makes clear statements about mandatory monetary benefits and voluntary monetary and non monetary benefits. Like the CBD, the ITPGRFA expressly states that the monetary and non-monetary benefits must be provided in a material transfer agreement (MTA).

MTA are provided under Part IV (Multilateral System on Access Benefit Sharing) of the ITPGRFA. The relevant provisions are Articles 10(1) and 10(2). These two provisions set the basis of sMTA. The former provision states that access regimes are to be developed by States through national legislation. The latter provision however, states that although such rights is in the preview of States, they must tailor their laws to facilitate the attainment of the intentions of the multilateral system relating to the efficient, effective and transparent access to Appendix 1 PGRFA. The provision also calls for the equitable sharing of the benefits arising from the utilization of the plant genetic resources on a complimentary and mutually reinforcing basis.

Article 12 spells out the conditions for access. First, it states that legal and natural persons may facilitate access under the jurisdiction of any party. Article 12(3) focuses on the conditions of access. The first condition is that access should only be allowed if it for research relating to conservation, breeding, and training for food and agriculture. If the application is for chemical, pharmaceutical, and non food or feed industries, access should be denied.

The second condition is that if access is granted, it should be done expeditiously and free of charge. However, when there is a fee charged, it must not exceed the minimum cost involved. The third condition is that upon receiving the PGRFA and where developments have been done on it, IPR should not be taken on them. However, when a PGRFA is under development, it is the discretion of the farmer to supply it. If however, IPR has already been taken on a PGRFA then they should be subject to national and international laws and therefore it would appear that access would be subject to these conditions. When the PGRFA has been accessed, it remains in the multilateral system and therefore parties may apply for its access as well.

Elements of sMTA[22]

Article 12.4 of the ITPGRFA stipulates that a MTA must facilitate the ABS arrangements between parties that are providing and receiving PGRFA in Appendix 1. This Article also states that a sMTA must facilitate access according to Article 12(2) and 12(3) and benefit sharing according to Article 13(2)(d)(ii) and other relevant provisions of the treaty.

Generally a sMTA will contain the following elements:

---

[22] The sMTA is still under negotiations at the time of drafting this paper and therefore the text is taken from the 1st Hammamet Contact Group meeting of the sMTA in August 1005.

- Preamble
- Identification of the parties to the agreement
- Definitions
- Subject matter of the MTA
- General provisions
- Rights and obligations of the provider
- Rights and obligations of the recipient
- Applicable law
- Dispute settlement
- Additional items
- Signature
- Appendix

The key elements of the sMTA are: (1) subject matter of the MTA; (2) rights and obligations of provider; and (3) the rights and obligations of recipient. The subject matter of the MTA defines the parameters of the sMTA. It identifies the crops in Appendix 1 of the ITPGRFA that the provider may transfer to the recipient and the type of benefit sharing arrangement that will apply. Under the sub-heading, rights and obligations of provider, the provider is required to supply (subject to national law) unconditionally passport data and other related information to the recipient. Some of the information that the provider must supply include:

- information expeditiously and when fee charged, not burdensome;
- available passport data;
- under development discretion of developer;
- IPR protection internationally and nationally; and
- notify third party beneficiary.

Under the sub-heading, rights and obligations of the recipient, the recipient may obtain the following rights and duties:

- plant genetic resource only for research;
- IPR should not be a barrier;
- use IPR if it conforms with IPR national laws;
- IPR can be taken on materials derived from the multilateral system, but must inform third party beneficiary;
- use IPR by conforming with national and international laws;
- if conserves material, inform multilateral system;
- if enters into new sMTA, no obligations if transferred to other party;
- consult country of origin when plant genetic resource transferred;
- subject to other provisions of sMTA, commercialization may occur
- provide for monetary arrangements; and

- share information and possibly technology.

The plant genetic resource that is the subject of the sMTA may be specified in an annexure to the sMTA. The specific components of benefits and how it should be shared may also be specified by an annexure to the sMTA.

Application of ITPGRFA in PNG

When dealing with issues of PGRFA in PNG, the National Agricultural Research Institute (NARI) takes prominence. This is because NARI is the 'custodians of these resources'. Also according to s 4(e) of the *National Agriculture and Research Institute Act*, NARI must maintain and conserve the diversity of genetic resources for food and agriculture, and also act as custodian for these resources and promote the effective utilization of these resources in this country. Drawing from this legal mandate, NARI is currently focused on three (3) major activities relating to ITPGRFA. These are:

1. obtaining PGRFA through PNG farmers or through field collections in PNG where research and development culminates in a new variety that is new and innovative;
2. PGRFA obtained through a provider outside PNG for the sole use of conservation and supply to farmers and wider community; and
3. PGRFA obtained through a provider outside PNG for developing varieties to improve existing varieties.

In the first activity NARI and PNG farmers become the provider of the new variety (PGRFA). There is however, no protection for NARI and PNG farmers' in terms of IPR. There are moves being in the legal system to develop an IPR arrangement for PGRFA. In the development of an IPR regime, a critical issue for consideration is this: when IPR is granted, what would be the scope of licensing fees given the general rules relating to access fees under the ITPGRFA? The issue of licensing fees should not be confused with mandatory monetary benefit sharing. They are two separate matters and should be considered as such. Because licensing fees are regulated by the ITPGRFA, the sMTA should focus on the revenue generated from the sale of the PGRFA. These sales should be used to determine the compulsory monetary benefits.

In the second activity, NARI (recipient) seeks to collaborate with external partners (providers) for the distribution and supply of PGRFA to PNG farmers and the wider community. The major concern NARI has with this activity is the charging of fees for the sole purpose of recovering administrative costs. A clear distinction must be made between fees as provided under the ITPGRFA and fees for cost recovery. Because the 'supplied' PGRFA is not being commercialized, NARI does not receive additional income from its distribution to farmers, it actually incurs costs in distributing the PGRFA. Such fees should therefore not be subject to the mandatory monetary benefits.

In the third activity, NARI (recipient) obtains a PGRFA from an external partner (provider) and develops a new PGRFA (provider) to improve existing varieties in PNG to tackle food security issues. In this activity, the NARI as the recipient develops a plant variety derived from the PGRFA and takes IPR protection on its innovation and as such, applies IPR monopoly on the PGRFA. Is this IPR monopoly contrary to the spirit of the ITPGRFA? This issue is by far the most controversial and has not yet been settled by NARI.

Assuming PNG does have IPR over varieties in activities 1 and 3, the scope of licensing will determine the level of access. It is suggested that the scope of licensing should enable full licensing so that access to the materials are given and a certain level of exclusivity is rendered. The danger with this proposition is that the cost of obtaining the PGRFA will be expensive, contrary to the ITPGRFA. However, given the rights of State to readjust fees, PNG can present a case for charging higher fees.

It is recommended that full licensing in activity 3 should encourage full disclosure of materials and associated technology. Also licensing fees should be discounted as the PGRFA would be in the multilateral system.

These three (3) activities would usually be catered by a sMTA. In terms of compulsory monetary benefit sharing arrangements under the sMTA, the following would have to be considered:

- Commercial sales where the intention is to profit from the sale of a PGRFA to a consumer;
- Recurrent sales where the intention is to recover the cost of importing the PGRF as well as maintenance costs in facilitating the PGRFA;
- Licensing from patent holder to the recipient whereby the scope of the license may determine the fee, that is, partial or full licensing. Apart from the variation of the fees, the rights and duties will also vary according to the scope of the license.

ABS and TRIPS

TRIPS is derived from Annex 1C of the Marrakesh Agreement that establishes the Multilateral Trading System of the World Trade Organization. It sets out minimum standards on trade related aspects of intellectual property rights. It does this through preserving the concept of monopoly ownership of IPR where the following principles are intended to be preserved:

- Reward or encourage creativeness;
- Reward and encourage research and development – investments;
- Protect consumers;
- Fair competition; and
- Balance of rights and obligations.

TRIPS enables the IPR holder monopoly for the distribution of the product to maximise the reward for creativity and at the same time recoup investments on R&D and also enable reinvestment in improving the process or product. IPR also protects consumers in the sense that reliability and efficiency of a particular product or process is recognised through features of the IPR. Without IPR, consumers cannot be assured of the reliability of the process or product.

Trade Related IPR on Copyrights and Patents

There are a number of trade related IPR, however, for ABS, the important ones are patents and to a lesser degree, copyright. Patents and copyright play an important role in both access and benefit sharing. Copyright is associated with information sharing and has a direct bearing on Article 17 of the CBD which relates to exchange of information. A close reading of Article 17 shows that copyright cannot be used to negate exchange of information under the CBD.

Patents attract a higher degree of protection. For present purposes, Article 27 (3) of TRIPS is imperative. Article 27(3)(b) stipulates that members may exclude from patentability:

> … plants and animals other then micro-organisms, and essentially biological processes from production of plants or animals other then non–biological and microbiological processes. However, members shall provide protection of plant varieties either by patents or by an effective sui generis system or by any combination thereof.

Effectively what this provision means is that plants and animals are not patentable. However, micro-organisms, non-biological processes and microbiological processes can be patented. This would suggest that genetic resources are patentable. What genetic resources would qualify for patenting is debatable. It is nevertheless clear that plant varieties may be protected by an effective *sui generis* system or patented or a combination of both.

Article 27 (3)(b) is critical in the sense that it recognizes two systems that may be used to protect genetic materials and contribute to access and at the same time offer benefit sharing in the monetary sense. The first is patents while the other is an effective *sui generis* system.

When considering patenting genetic materials, the following can be observed. The absence of an internationally accepted definition of 'invention' has proved to be problematic and has given rise to varying practices on patenting of genetic material. For example, genetic materials may be patented in the United States if its biological resources are claimed in isolated form (suggesting biological discoveries of a particular genetic function is patentable, such as in the Hagahai case[23]). On the other hand, in Brazil and the Andean Group, a genetic material must be modified in order to be patentable. In PNG, the *Patents and Industrial Designs Act* provides a clear definition of 'invention' which excludes the patenting of genetic resources.

When considering an effective *sui generis* system for plant varieties, it must be noted that TRIPS envisages a system that provides IPR based on a simple criteria. Thus, a mere plant variety developed through a conventional breeding by making one plant have different foliages to another can be protected through a *sui generis* system.

ABS and International Trade

ABS is significant for international trade because of the commercialization of a process or product which was developed as a result of research and development relating to a genetic resource. At this stage, it is generally accepted that IPR had been obtained on the relevant process or product and that the process or product is now operating within the multilateral trading system. The process or product now becomes a trade in good for the purposes of commercialization and international trade. Two important issues emerge at this juncture and may act as barriers to the successful commercialization of the process or product. These two issues are tariff and non-tariff barriers. For present purposes, the latter issue is more important particularly as it relates to sanitary and phytosanitary (SPS) measures, as well as technical barriers to trade (TBT).

Both the SPS and the TBT are part of the Agreement on Goods in Annex 1A of the Marrakesh Agreement. They are respectively referred to as the SPS Agreement and the TBT Agreement.

SPS Agreement and Trade in Goods Derived and ABS

The SPS Agreement combines 3 main principles of SPS protection:

- International Plant Protection Convention (plant);
- Office of Epizootics (animals); and
- Human protection (human).

[23] See Kwa, note 1.

The SPS protections builds upon the existing convention on plant protection from harmful trade in goods that effects plant life, the office of epizootics which protects animals and human protection based on quarantine practices. The level of protection is based on scientific standards. A process or product derived from the manipulation of a genetic material obtained through an ABS arrangement, must meet these scientific standards, before it can be commercialized. Failure to meet these standards will render the process or product unfit for consumption and as such, will not be able to be traded in the markets.

An important treaty that has close affinity to the SPS Agreement is the Cartagena Protocol on Biosafety. Safety measures relating to genetically modified organisms established under the Protocol must also comply with the SPS Agreement. The nature of the relationship between the two different standards provided under these two agreements are still be debated at the international level.

TBT Agreement and Trade in Goods Derived from an ABS Arrangement

Like the SPS Agreement, the TBT Agreement focuses on standards for consumer protection. The standards however relate to technical industrial standards. The potential process or product that will be traded must met the safety and operational standards to be certified as fit for consumption. These standards are usually adopted from the International Standards Organization (ISO).

Thus, a process or product developed from a genetic material obtained under an ABS arrangement would have to meet all the TBT standards before being commercialized. TBT standards will apply to the laboratory, to those who work in the laboratory and the techniques used for mass production. Like the SPS standards, if these TBT standards are not met, the potential process or product cannot be traded in the markets.

Summary

The review provided in this Chapter shows that the CBD does not adequately address ABS apart from the general statements under Article 15. Articles 16-21 provide mere guidelines on ABS. These provisions however provide useful guide in the formulation of an ABS framework.

The other three (3) treaties (UNCLOLS, ITPGRFA and TRIPS) that were reviewed also do not adequately deal with ABS relating to genetic resources. Based on the information gleaned from the four (4) treaties, the following principles emerge:

- Granting Access is the sovereign right of the State;
- Rules relating to access must not be harsh and oppressive;

- Access can be for the genetic material;
- Access can be for traditional knowledge;
- Access can be for scientific knowledge;
- Access to genetic material existing IPR must be adhered to and therefore compliance of its operations must be given;
- Benefit sharing can be restricted to either monetary or non monetary benefits or a combination of both;
- Monetary benefits are can be in the form of access fees; one off compensation payment; or licensing fees through patents;
- Non-monetary benefits can consist of technology transfer through the physical transfer of equipment, or information associated with the improvement of the genetic material or TK or scientific knowledge; and
- Commercialization of a process or product derived from genetic material obtained through an ABS arrangement depends on its compliance with existing SPS and TBT standards for the process or product to be traded in the markets.

An ABS regulatory framework must incorporate these principles to enable it to stand up to international standards.

Chapter 4. Access and Benefit Sharing: Some Principles for Consideration

Enaha P Kwa

Introduction

ABS is one of the two notable mechanisms promoted by the Convention on Biological Diversity. The other is Prior Informed Consent. This Chapter will focus on ABS in particular benefit sharing and its relevance to PNG. A significant part of the discussion will focus on the concept of participation. This Chapter identifies and highlights the pivotal role that participation can and should play in: (1) identifying benefits; (2) identifying beneficiaries; and (3) ensuring the fair and equitable distribution of benefits. In PNG, benefit sharing is still in the embryonic stage of development. It has even been said that benefit sharing and distribution has contributed to increasing enclaves of poverty in resource development projects. The development of an ABS framework must therefore lead to the alleviation of poverty where it exists, and also improve the livelihood of the people or communities who own, manage or are affected by the actions of external agents who might benefit as a part of any of the activities covered by the Convention on Biological Diversity.

Thematic Areas of the CBD and Access Benefit Sharing

The themes covered by the CBD integrate all the problems faced on a national scale and allow the formulation of achievable measurable actions. The following are the twenty (20) key themes that have been identified so far:

1. Access and Benefit Sharing
2. Protected Areas
3. Biosafety
4. Criteria and Indicators
5. Agrobiodiversity
6. Forest Biodiversity
7. Mountain Biodiversity
8. Marine and Coastal Biodiversity
9. Inland Water Ecosystems

10. Dryland Ecosystems
11. Species and Taxonomy
12. Impact Assessment
13. Incentive Measures
14. Biodiversity Legal Issues
15. Capacity Building
16. Traditional Knowledge
17. Biodiversity Funding Sources
18. Synergy with Rio Conventions and Other Biodiversity Conventions
19. Sustainable Tourism
20. Sustainable Use of Biodiversity.

As part of the challenge in implementing the CBD, a theoretical framework was developed by ecologist Benoit Gauthier.[24] The theoretical framework called the 'Biodiversity Planning Matrix' was designed to assist biodiversity planners to capture the relevant information needed to implement the various aspects of the CBD, including ABS. For present purposes, this matrix will be discussed in relation to benefit sharing and then adapted towards designing a benefit sharing framework for PNG. The planning matrix theme areas are arranged in Activity Sectors. These activity sectors are:

1. Energy Resources
2. Conservation of Natural Resources
3. Development of Wildlife Resources
4. Development of Forest Resources
5. Development of Agriculture Resources
6. Development of Mineral Resources
7. Industrial Development of Technology and Services
8. Development of the Urban and Rural Environment
9. Atmospheric and Aquatic Basins
10. Territories under Special Jurisdiction
11. Environment and Civil Emergencies
12. Eco-civism (Civil society participation)
13. Societal Values
14. Quality of Life
15. Spiritual and Religious Values

The planning matrix theme areas that may incorporate Access and Benefits Sharing are: activity sectors 2, 3, 4, 5, 7, 12, 13 and 14. Eight (8) of the fifteen (15) sectors identify Access Benefit Sharing as a key theme to increasing the security of biodiversity in that sector. This indicates that benefit sharing is a significant consideration or deciding factor in many activity sectors. In developing a benefit sharing regime, the aim is to ensure

---

[24] Prescott (2000), p9.

that the benefit sharing process results in an increasing level of intangible and tangible benefits in the different stages of implementation rather than exclusively focus on increasing the monetary value for stakeholders.

Benefits and Beneficiaries

Benefit sharing exists in a pyramid structure, where the most number of beneficiaries initially benefit, but a significantly smaller number benefit when the activity is at its most profitable. The primary challenge is to allow access for the most number of beneficiaries to benefit (more tangible and intangible benefits) throughout the lifespan of the activity.

Benefit Sharing has been difficult primarily because it depends, firstly, on the amount of monetary benefits being transferred, secondly, on the types of benefits, and thirdly, on the beneficiaries.

Volume of monetary benefits

The volume of monetary benefits depends on the size of the market for products based on genetic resources, and on the willingness of consumers to pay for those products. There are some estimates regarding market size, the best known being based on a large industry survey by Kate and Laird, who calculate the size of the market at between US$ 500 and 800 billion. While this figure indicates the consumptive direct use value in industrialized countries, they do not permit a reliable appraisal of consumers' willingness to pay for genetic resources incorporated in end products. This is even more difficult where genetic resources are intended for future use. Empirical and anecdotal evidence suggests that willingness to pay is not very pronounced, since industry prefers to substitute synthetic inputs for genetic resources. The few reports of ABS agreements refer to no more than small amounts of monetary transfers being received and to future royalty commitments ranging between 1-5% of product sales. Apart from isolated success stories, monetary benefits will therefore be insufficient to compensate provider countries for the opportunity costs of biodiversity conservation or to increase the economic capabilities of the poor more than marginally.

Types of benefits

Some benefits increase *opportunities* for the poor, while others contribute to their *empowerment.* Opportunities may be increased by direct monetary transfers, by investment in capital and by generating additional investment in the most important asset, human capital (e.g. through training). Positive as this is, it should be noted that transfers of this sort may well give rise to conflicts at local level, since many transfers generate private (exclusive) benefits rather than public goods. The more valuable genetic resources become, the greater is the danger that the local poor will be deprived of the private benefits that could enhance their opportunities.

ABS agreements can generate non-monetary benefits that empower the local poor. If properly designed, the negotiations process should involve as many local and indigenous communities and the contract should cater for the interests of the local communities. The important point here is that the ABS process gives the local and indigenous communities a *right* to participate, thus making their voice heard.

Beneficiaries

Different stakeholders such as local and indigenous communities, governments, industry, and researchers can benefit, however only some are poor.

Local and indigenous communities: This group of stakeholders will probably form part of the poorer segments of the providing country. Benefits that are directly targeted at this group are therefore likely to have a poverty-alleviating effect by directly increasing their economic opportunities. Income generation may be possible through the sharing of monetary benefits or through short-term monetary benefits (e.g. for guides or for the cultivation of biological resources that are traded for their genetic properties). Future assets could be improved through investment in training or basic infrastructure. Benefit sharing can empower local and indigenous communities if the national governments of providing countries give them a say in the negotiation of the initial negotiations and the final contract.

Government: Most governments will be interested in monetary benefits as a source of income for the national budget. The contents of ABS agreements are determined by the public policies of the government: if they are pro-poor, additional government spending is most welcome as a means of improving services for the poor. However, if the government does not concern itself with the poor, the sharing of monetary benefits will contribute little to poverty reduction.

Industry and science: Most providing countries seek to develop their own industrial or scientific capacities through the use of their genetic resources. They are therefore interested in technology transfer and capacity-building. Although this will primarily benefit the middle class in the short term, the strategy may help to increase the economic opportunities of the poor in the long term, firstly, by fostering economic growth and, secondly, by increasing the national market in biodiversity related products.

Finally, the beneficiaries of biodiversity are not limited to the present time. As Table 2 shows, beneficiaries of biodiversity are not restricted to direct beneficiaries but also to indirect beneficiaries, such as future generations.

Table 2: *Beneficiaries of Biodiversity on a Spatial and Temporal Scale*

	List of Beneficiaries	**Beneficiaries at a global level**
Present	*Direct use level:* -Poor rural level, farmers, medicinal purposes. -Workers in the tourism country	*Direct use value:* -Consumers of herbal medicines and related industries, mostly in industrialized countries. -Tourists
	Indirect use value: -Farmers (stability of local ecosystem)	*Indirect use value:* -Upstream users of land and energy in developing countries; world community (eg. through carbon storage function)
	Existence Value: -Local communities and indigenous peoples owing cultural beliefs.	*Existence value:* -Environment lobbies and concerned people.
Future	*Existence value:* -Local communities and indigenous peoples owing cultural beliefs. (heritable value)	*Existence value:* -Environment lobbies and concerned people. (heritable value)
	Indirect value: -Future farmers using a stable environment.	*Indirect value:* -Future generations using ecosystem functions.
		Option value: -Future consumers interested in the global gene pool, mostly in industrialized countries.

Source: Prescott (2003)

Therefore the potential of benefit sharing that may be derived from biodiversity covers a broad spectrum, ranging from the present to the future, direct and indirect benefits, existence value, option value, monetary and non-monetary, tangible and the non-tangible.

Biodiversity and Poverty

The relationship between ABS and poverty is multi-dimensional in that while poverty may undermine biodiversity, the poor may at the same time depend on biodiversity. The World Bank definition of poverty is the "pronounced deprivation in well-being". At the root of "deprivation" lie numerous mutually reinforcing dimensions of poverty including: lack of income to meet basic needs; vulnerability to external shocks; and the absence of opportunities to influence public institutions. More recently, new dimensions of poverty (other than income measures) such as exposure to risk, voicelessness and powerlessness have emerged. In this broad sense then, poverty restricts the "capabilities that a person has, that is, the substantive freedoms he or she enjoys to lead the kind of life he or she values".

The major setback of poverty reduction strategies is that they are not able to adequately address all the dimensions of poverty which interact and frequently reinforce each other. The idea is to alleviate poverty by utilizing biodiversity resources that are present in a given community so as to ensure sustainability of that resource in its natural environment. In Papua New Guinea, poverty alleviation has been identified and acknowledged as a priority development issue by the government in the MTDS 2005-2010, and by the United Nations in 'The Millennium Development Goals: Progress Report for Papua New Guinea 2004'. For Papua New Guinea, Access and Benefit Sharing is very important because of its potential to fundamentally change perceptions of benefits derived from the broader spectrum of development. Benefit sharing advocates equitable distribution of benefits to ensure that all beneficiaries benefit equally.

However, the poverty alleviating effect of benefit sharing is not simple because of the dependence on, firstly, the volume of monetary benefits, secondly, on the types of benefits, and thirdly, on the beneficiaries themselves. It is suggested that although the volume of monetary effects is limited, ABS can foster opportunities and empowerment for the poor over a sustained period of time. The Access and Benefit Sharing experiences of five cases studies the by German Development Institute[25] shown in Table 3 illustrate the complexities of achieving poverty alleviation. The biological resources used range from plants (*Kava, Kani, Hoodia, INBio*) to insects (*INBio*), marine invertebrates (*MSI-Cancer*), microorganisms (*InBio*) and market herbal botanicals for health care (*Kava, Kani, Hoodia*), with the lead substances being further optimized for use as biopharmaceuticals (*Hoodia*) or directly screened for biopharmaceutical leads (*INBio*, *MSI-Cancer*).

The *actors* are varied from pharmaceutical companies, companies dealing in herbal medicines, universities and biodiversity research institutions, indigenous and local communities to government agencies.

[25] Henne (2003), pp10 – 28.

Table 3: *Case Studies on Access and Benefit Sharing Agreements*

Case Study 1: The Kani Case (Kani)

Type of genetic resource: *Trichopus zeylanicus spp. travancoricus* (Trichopodaceae), a herbaceous, perennial, rhizomatous plant (local name: *argyapaacha*) found in the Agasthyar Hills of the Western Ghats (in Kerala and Tamil Nadu, India) that produces a rosette of 10 to 15 evergreen leaves weighing 100 to 200 g, with 2 or 3 flushes every year. It seems that only the subspecies found in Agasthyar has the claimed medicinal properties, although the species (*Trichopus zeylanicus*) is also found in the Malay peninsula and Sri Lanka.

Actors involved

1) The Kani people, originally a semi-nomadic tribal community, who now lead a largely settled life in the forests of the Thiruvananthapuram district of Kerala in the Western Ghats: the customary rights to transfer and use certain traditional medicinal knowledge are held by tribal healers, known as *Plathis*. This knowledge is traditionally passed on from one generation to another, for the most part orally.
2) The Tropical Botanic Garden and Research Institute (TBGRI), an autonomous institution set up in 1979 by the government of Kerala for research and development. It has the largest botanical garden in Asia, with a wide collection of tropical plant species. One of the Institute's main aims is to carry out botanical, chemical and pharmacological research for the development of scientifically validated and standardized herbal drugs.
3) Arya Vaidya Pharmacy Ltd (AVP), a private company based in Coimbatore, which has been engaged in manufacturing high quality Ayurvedic drugs since 1948.

How the genetic resource is used

The plant is eaten by the Kani people to suppress fatigue and reduce stress. On the basis of this traditional knowledge, which was revealed by a number of Kani guides to members of a TBGRI expedition in 1987, the TBGRI spent seven to eight years carrying out all the investigations, toxicity tests and clinical trials needed to complete the formulation of *Jeevani*, a herbal drug consisting of four compounds. Subsequently, the TBGRI obtained a national process patent for *Jeevani* and licensed the product in November 1995 to Arya Vaidya Pharmacy Ltd for seven years at a licence fee of US$ 25,000 and a 2% royalty on ex-factory sales for ten years from the date on which commercial production began. In 2000, NutriScience Innovations LLC, a US-based supplier of nutritional and functional food ingredients registered the trademark *Jeevani* for the sale of the same drug in the USA. Jeevani is also an ingredient of the energizer Adrenerlin and is included in such Chinese/Japanese medicines as "Shosaikoto" to considerable clinical effect. Jeevani, based, as it is, on the Kani tribe's traditional knowledge, seems to have tremendous potential in the global natural health care product and sports medicine markets.

ABS agreement

The idea of sharing the licence fee and royalties obtained from AVP was developed by the TBGRI with a view to recognizing Kani's contribution, rather than as a result of any legal obligation to enter into such a benefit-sharing arrangement. At the time, there was no defined structure or policy in India for the sharing of benefits between originator communities and other bodies involved in the use of traditional community knowledge. In 1997, with the help of the TBGRI, NGOs and local government officials, the Kerala Kani Samudaya Kshema Trust was founded to represent Kani communities and promote local development in a unique and unprecedented benefit-sharing arrangement in India.

Implementation and compliance instruments

As the benefit-sharing agreement with the Kani is voluntary and based on a decision of the TBGRI Board of Directors, there are no legally binding instruments to ensure implementation and compliance by the TBGRI. The licence agreement between the TBGRI and Arya Vaidya Pharmacy Ltd is governed by Indian civil law.

Benefits

The TBGRI agreed to give to the tribal community 50% of the licence fee and 50% of the royalties obtained by AVP from the sale of Jeevani.

Benefits realized to date: In March 1999, the amount due to the Kerala Kani Samudaya

Welfare Trust by that time (US$ 12,500, i.e. its 50% share of the licence fee) was transferred to the trust on the understanding that only the interest accruing from this amount would be used for the welfare activities of the Kani tribe. It has been impossible to realize any further benefits in the meantime, since the Forest Department, which has jurisdiction over the forest areas in which the Kani have settled, does not allow the plant to be collected or cultivated, even though cultivation methods allowing sustainable harvesting have been developed by the TBGRI together with the Kani. The Kani are thus prevented from delivering sufficient plant material to Arya Vaidya Pharmacy.

Indirect benefits: The TBGRI has also trained dozens of tribal families to cultivate the plant around their dwellings in the forest. In the first year of cultivation, before cultivation of the plant was stopped by the Kerala Forest Department in late 1999, each family earned about Rs 8,000 (about US$ 180) from the sale of *arogyaapacha* leaves. Representing over 700 families, the Trust began to provide a critical source of employment for tribal people as cultivators and processors of the plant, while ensuring that harvesting techniques were sustainable.

Direct contribution to poverty reduction

So far, the Trust has supported poor members of the community, provided insurance for pregnant women and assisted when accidents have occurred. As soon as the Kerala Forest Department approves the cultivation of *arogyaapacha*, the Kani will be able to develop a regular source of income based on the sustainable use of the natural resources of the forests they inhabit. This will help to empower communities to become involved in the conservation and development of the natural resources for their own benefit and that of the wider world. The agreement between the TBGRI and the Kani triggered a discussion among the Kani themselves on the inherent value and custodianship of their traditional knowledge, and this has led to self-organization and a general recognition of the individual responsibility of tribal members for the welfare of the whole community.

Lessons learnt to date

The Kani, who number about 17,000, live in different areas and have differing opinions on the arrangement with the TBGRI, which in the early stages in particular interacted primarily with the Kani from one area. This group of Kani supports and appreciates the TBGRI's role. However, Kani in other areas were offended by the restriction of the TBGRI's cooperation to one group – the one which revealed the knowledge considered sacred by some members of the community. The TBGRI acknowledged that it had not reached out to or communicated with all members of the Kani tribe, and the Trust was therefore established and registered with initially about 500 members. Today it represents over 700 families with a much broader regional coverage than at the outset. The TBGRI process for the sharing of benefits with the Kani evolved in a policy vacuum, well before the CBD was introduced. The lessons learnt from mistakes made in this case did not have the luxury of a precedent or of guiding legislation passed by the national government. Instead, procedures were developed gradually in an *ad hoc* manner over the years. This occurred despite the fact that all project participants were nationals, with no international trade, companies or institutions involved. From the TBGRI's perspective, the whole effort was based on mutual trust and benefit between itself and the Kani. The ratification of the CBD by the Government of India in February 1994, however, helped to implement the benefit-sharing scheme with the Kani despite the efforts of the Tribal Welfare Department of India to block it. This case highlights the need for multi-stakeholder frameworks to discuss the scale of access, value addition and benefit-sharing. If the Forest Department has jurisdiction over a territory, it must be included in the stakeholder discussions while benefit-sharing mechanisms are being established. Under the existing IPR regime, the scale of the benefits to be shared could have been much wider if:

- international patent applications had been filed under the Patent Cooperation Treaty administered by WIPO,
- to protect formulation in countries other than India,
- produce patents rather than mere process patents had been available in India for pharmaceutical products, trademarks had been registered to protect the features that distinguish this product from those of other undertakings.

Case Study 2: The Kava case *(Kava)*

Type of genetic resource: *Piper methysticum* (Piperaceae), a perennial shrub growing to 3 m, with bright green, heart-shaped leaves about 15 to 20 cm in length. Kava is the ceremonial and social drink of several Pacific island nations, and its cultivation, properties and uses have become a central part of Pacific island traditional knowledge. The plant has also been the subject of research and commercialization by Western researchers and firms since the middle of the 19th century. The medicinal and sedative properties of kava are well documented, and today there are a growing number of kava-based preparations in the European and US markets, some of which have been patented.

Actors involved

1) Traditional and commercial kava growers in the Pacific islands.
2) Numerous companies in the herbal industry, which have filed patent claims relating to the processing, preparation and use of kava. They include the French companies L'Oréal (EP 0672046) and Sederma S.A. (WO 9925369), Germany's Willmar Schwabe (DE 4028945) and Japan's Lion Corp (JP 1007464) and Shiseido (JP 09067238).

How the genetic resource is used

Kava plays an important role in the culture and social customs of the region. It has been cultivated for over 3,000 years and is used by Pacific islanders in religious ceremonies, in courtship rituals and at social gatherings. More than 118 cultivars are known to have been developed by farmers. It is a mood-altering substance, inducing relaxation, peace of mind and contentment, as well as a sharpening of the senses. Herbalists have traditionally used kava as a remedy for nervousness, urinary problems, asthma, whooping cough, stomach ache and headache. It is also used as a muscle relaxant for the relief of spasms and cramp. Kava is traditionally used in herbal medicines in non-standardized preparations, and no negative effects are reported. The active compounds of kava are found in the rootstock. They consist primarily of the kavalactones, fifteen of which have been isolated. To date, scientific studies have identified three as responsible for a range of medicinal activities: dihydromethysticin (DHM), dihydrokavain (DHK) and kavain. Demonstrated activities include the inducement of sleep, painkilling, local anaesthetic, anti-convulsive, and anti-bacterial activity. The activity of kava is determined by the kavalactone content and absorption, which depend on the variety and maturity of the plant, how it is prepared and processed and how it is consumed.

ABS agreement: none.

Implementation and compliance instruments: not relevant.

Benefits

Benefits realized to date: not relevant.

Indirect benefits: Kava is among the ten best-selling herbs globally. A boom in 1998 saw sales surge to an estimated US$ 50 million. While only about 100,000 kg was shipped to Europe in the whole of 1996, Fiji alone exported 50,000 kg of dried roots every week in 1998. In 1997, kava extract was sold by processing companies to manufacturers for US$ 100 per kg, compared to US$ 250 to 300 per kg in 1998. The dramatic increase in the popularity of kava during the second half of the 1990s caused demand temporarily to outstrip supply. Good-quality material has usually sold out within a few days. A recent downturn in demand in the US and European herbal markets, influenced by adverse media coverage, led to a drastic slump, with unfavourable effects on local economies and growers, who had been increasing the acreage under cultivation. Marketing and export businesses have suffered. One small consolation for farmers is that the domestic market is strong and expanding and that the use of kava for traditional purposes and its cultural symbolism have grown. There are now kava bars, and kava is used symbolically in Christian atonement.

Direct contribution to poverty reduction
The use of kava by the herbal industry has the potential to contribute significantly to poverty reduction. Small farmers could earn substantial income from the cultivation of kava. However, market structures and marketing channels stand in the way of small farmers obtaining a fair share of the end product's value. This is true not only of kava but also of many other botanical resources of the herbal industry, such as devil's claw, *Harpagophytum procumbens* and *Harpagophytum zeyherii* (Pedaliaceae), from southern Africa and cohune, *Orbignya cohune* (Arecaceae), from Central America. As the kava case demonstrates, international recognition of a local natural resource may lead to its local recognition and so to increased local demand, thus ensuring additional employment and income possibilities for local growers.

Lessons learnt to date
Kava is a major cash crop in the Pacific islands. However, substantial cultivation may eventually be developed elsewhere. World Botanicals (US) and others are looking at kava cultivation in the US state of Hawaii, the French colony of New Caledonia, Queensland in northern Australia and even Mexico. Kava from Hawaii is beginning to come on to the market in significant quantities, and as countries with a far larger acreage

to sow than the small Pacific islands emerge with their kava harvests, the premium currently enjoyed by a few states seems certain to disappear. US and European companies have trademarked a number of terms related to kava, including the names "Kava Pure" and "Kavatril." There are also at least five patents on kava extracts and active compounds. At least one company has obtained a patent on a combination of kava and other herbs, "Kavatrol". Kava appears to be a product with significant potential for the use of trademarks or geographical indications. An appropriate trademark, particularly a certification mark that reflected standards of environmental and socially responsible sourcing and processing of raw materials, might very well increase the Pacific growers' market share if they could identify or develop suitable local cultivars that could be marketed as "True Kava"(™). This would be similar to the *Appellation of Origin* (DOC) label attached to some European wines and cheeses, which gives recognition to long histories of community-based innovation and experimentation that have resulting in the products we buy today. Measures needed to secure such an appellation for kava might include the use of clearly defined varieties and processing methods, all adequately monitored, with labeled products for each country. This may go some way to encourage quality control and social and environmental standards.

Case Study 3 The Hoodia case (*Hoodia*)

Type of genetic resource: *Hoodia gordonii* (Asclepiadaceae), a succulent plant about 45 cm tall and indigenous to southern Africa.

Actors involved

1) The San (Kalahari bushmen), one of the most poverty-stricken and marginalized communities in the region, live in Angola, Namibia, Botswana and South Africa and are organized in the Working Group of Indigenous Minorities in Southern Africa (WIMSA) and the South African San Council.
2) The Council for Scientific and Industrial Research (CSIR), a South African-based statutory board which represents one of the largest research organizations in Africa, responsible for 12% of all industrial research and development on the continent.
3) Phytopharm plc, a small British pharmaceutical company, specializing in the development of phytomedicines, founded 1990.
4) Pfizer Inc., a US-based multinational life science corporation.

How the genetic resource is used

The Hoodia cactus has long been used by the San to stave off hunger and thirst. In 1995 the CSIR patented Hoodia's appetite-suppressing element (P57). In 1997 it licensed P57 to Phytopharm. In 1998, an exclusive world-wide licensing agreement was signed by Phytopharm and Pfizer for the development and global commercialization of P57 as an oral prescription drug for the treatment of obesity (a market worth more than US$ 10 billion). Phytopharm will receive up to US$ 32 million in royalty and milestone payments. P57 is considered to have the potential to become a "blockbuster" drug and is likely to be commercialized as a prescription medicine with an estimated market potential of US$ 1 to 8 billion.

ABS agreement

With the consent of the Department of Environmental Affairs and Tourism (DEAT), the CSIR has developed a bioprospecting agreement with Phytopharm under the law of contract with a view to providing DEAT with case studies as a basis for future policy development. Under a 2002 Memorandum of Understanding with the South African San Council, the CSIR has formally recognized the San as the originators of traditional knowledge associated with the human use of Hoodia. March 2003 saw the conclusion of negotiations between the San and CSIR on the specifics of a mutually acceptable benefit-sharing agreement. In the event of successful commercialization, the potential income stream will be deposited in the San Hoodia Benefit Sharing Trust, established by the CSIR and the South African San Council to improve the standard of living and well-being of the San peoples of southern Africa. The Trust will include representatives of the CSIR, the =Khomani, !Xun and Khwe, other San stakeholders in southern Africa, the WIMSA and the Department of Science and Technology, with strict rules determining the distribution of funds to beneficiaries. The agreement commits the parties to conserving biodiversity, requires the CSIR to grant the San access to existing study bursaries and, significantly, lays the foundations for further collaboration in bioprospecting.

Implementation and compliance instruments

A contract governed by South African law.

Benefits

Benefit-sharing is agreed in the contract as a two-step procedure. As the first step, the CSIR receives milestone payments and royalties from Pfizer and Phytopharm. By licensing the technology, the CSIR is likely to earn US$ 10 million in milestone payments, linked to the success of the drug at different stages of the clinical trials. The specific royalty percentage has not been made public, but is considered by the CSIR to be substantial by international standards. Typically, royalty percentages for pharmaceuticals range from 0.5% to 5% of total sales. If successful, the commercialization of P57 is likely to bring in tens of millions of US$ p.a. in royalty income for the CSIR during the life of the patent (15 to 20 years). As the second step, the CSIR will pay the San 8% of all milestone payments it receives from its licensee, as well as 6% of all royalties that the CSIR receives once the drug is commercially available. Milestone payments are subject to agreed technical performance targets for P57 during its clinical development over the next three to four years, and royalties are based on sales, which are not scheduled to begin before 2008. The San will thus receive only a very small proportion – less than 0.03% – of net proceeds from the sale of the product. Owing to this two-step procedure, Pfizer and Phytopharm are exempted from sharing the benefits directly with the San. As the CSIR acts as an intermediary, the San depend on its negotiating strategy for their share of the benefits. Moreover, the agreement stipulates that the companies are protected against any further financial demands from the San. It also explicitly prevents the San from using their knowledge of Hoodia in any other commercial applications.

Benefits realized to date: So far, US$ 33,000 has been paid into the San Hoodia Benefit Sharing Trust as the San's share of the milestone payments received by the CSIR.

Indirect benefits: Two of the more significant indirect benefits to emanate from the agreement have been the construction of a medicinal plant extraction facility at the CSIR, which requires the approval of the US Food & Drug Administration and manufactures material used in P57 clinical trials, and the establishment of a Botanical Supplies Unit – each the first of its kind in the world. Where the San are concerned, what is most remarkable is that the benefit-sharing agreement covers not only the San living in South Africa but the San community throughout southern Africa. This strengthens the cross-border identification of the San as an indigenous people of southern Africa and may do a great deal to improve the position of San communities in some of the other countries, where they are even more marginalized than in South Africa and Namibia and are fighting for recognition by the various national governments.

Direct contribution to poverty reduction

The funds received by the trust will be used to improve the general living conditions of the marginalized San communities in southern African countries through the development of health care, infrastructure and social security. In the long term the benefit-sharing agreement will help to further the recognition of the San as an indigenous people not only in South Africa but in the region as a whole. Currently, commercial farmers in the Northern Province and Northern Cape are undertaking cultivation trials. Further cultivation represents an obvious development opportunity for the San and other marginalized communities, although the technical challenges associated with the plant's cultivation are reportedly considerable. The scarcity of water also constrains cultivation in the parched areas of the Kalahari, where many of the San live. Successful cultivation will not only contribute to sustainable resource use but also provide income for local communities. Trade in herbal Hoodia products is growing, and demand will most probably increase in the coming years.

Lessons learnt to date

Many consider South Africa to have reached an important turning point in bioprospecting. Patent rights to the active constituents of Hoodia responsible for suppressing appetite have been successfully retained by South Africa through the CSIR (although other Hoodia-related patents remain foreign-owned), with foreign drug firms obtaining licences for the further development and commercialization of the drug. The 2002 Memorandum of Understanding between the CSIR and the South African San Council recognizes the San as the originators of the relevant knowledge. However, the agreement is almost entirely confined to monetary benefits, which hinge on product sales and successful commercialization. Yet commercialization is far from certain: Phytopharm announced on 30 July 2003 that it had been notified of Pfizer's decision to discontinue the clinical development of P57 for the treatment of obesity and to return the rights to Phytopharm. Following the closure of the Natureceuticals group within Pfizer, the company has decided that P57 may best be developed by another organization. As a result, Phytopharm is now free to license P57 to other parties. Pfizer also stated that clinical data on P57 in patients indicate the wisdom of further study of the use of the natural material in the treatment of obesity.

Case Study 4 The MSI anti-cancer agreement (*MSI-Cancer*)

Type of genetic resource: Marine organisms as a source of extracts and compounds with potential anti-cancer activity, originating from specific areas within the Philippine archipelago.

Actors involved

1) Marine Science Institute of the University of the Philippines (UP-MSI) – co-collector.
2) University of Utah, USA – principal collector.
3) Philippine Department of Agriculture (DA).
4) Wyeth-Ayerst, formerly American Cyanamid, USA – receives under a transfer agreement materials from the University of Utah for further research and commercialization.

How the genetic resource is used

The commercial research agreement (CRA), which is entitled "Anticancer Agents from Unique Natural Product Sources", allows the parties "to collect from certain areas in the Philippines marine organisms as a source of extracts and compounds with potential anticancer activity, which shall be exported to the United States for evaluation of the presence of the stated medicinal or pharmacological content."

ABS agreement

The CRA 98 – based on Presidential Executive Order 247 (EO 247) – between the Marine Science Institute of the University of the Philippines, the Department of Agriculture of the Philippines and the University of Utah, USA, was approved for three years in July 1998. The main objectives of the CRA 98 are: (1) to collect marine organisms from different habitats within the Philippine archipelago; (2) to isolate active metabolites and to determine their structure and (3) to perform systematic inventories of the biodiversity of the various habitats within the Philippine marine ecosystem. The agreement expired in 2001 and was renewed for another three years in 2002.

Implementation and compliance instruments

EO 247 became law on 18 May 1995 in response to a non-governmental initiative aimed at implementing the Convention on Biological Diversity. It provides a legal framework for bioprospecting and is one of the first attempts by a nation formally to regulate access to biological diversity. In June 1996, the Department of Environment and Natural Resources issued Department Administrative Order No 20 (DAO 96-20), which sets out the rules and regulations governing the implementation of EO 247. The joint obligations of CRA 98 require the collectors to comply with all the applicable laws and regulations of the Republic of the Philippines and the United States of America. Any controversy or dispute related to the agreement which cannot be settled by mutual accord between the parties must be settled by arbitration. The Department of Agriculture's obligations include the monitoring of the research activities to ensure compliance with the provisions of EO 247, DAO 96-20 and CRA 98. The collectors must submit a copy of the collection reports to the field office of the Department's Fisheries Office nearest the collection site. They must also provide the Department with a complete list of institutions, gene banks and other depositories where materials, data and documents have been placed. The Department of Agriculture has reserved the right to suspend or stop any collection or research activity if the collectors do not follow the prescribed Prior Informed Countries (PIC) process. Willful violation by the collectors of the terms and conditions of the agreement will result in its cancellation, the confiscation of the materials by the Philippine government and the imposition of reasonable penalties as provided under Section 10 of EO 247. The principal collector may rescind the agreement in the event of bankruptcy, security problems and *force majeure*, provided that, in the case of bankruptcy, all bonds are forfeited and all equipment and materials and related documents transferred to the co-collector and other Philippine institutions.

Benefits

An annual bioprospecting fee of PhP 10,000 (about US$ 200) payable to the Interagency Committee for Biological and Genetic Resources for the duration of the agreement. Additionally, a minimal performance bond no greater than PhP 10,000, which will be returned upon the termination of the agreement on condition that none of the provisions of the agreement has been violated. Five per cent of the net revenue received by the collectors in respect of any invention, licence, royalty or other commercialization of any material will be paid to the Department of Agriculture (the Integrated Protected Areas Fund, if the materials come from a protected area, the indigenous people or local community who gave the PIC or the individuals who provided such materials from private property). The two collectors have agreed in a memorandum to share equally (50/50) the intellectual property rights and any ensuing material benefits from discoveries made during this project. The UP-MSI is also required to help train government representatives in taxonomy or natural products chemistry under short-term internship programmes. The systematic inventories of the biodiversity of the various habitats within the Philippine marine ecosystem will increase knowledge of the biodiversity and conservation status of marine organisms. A complete set of all specimens is to be deposited at the UP-MSI, which will make arrangements with the National Museum of the Philippines regarding the requirement for holotypes. To provide benefits for the communities, the UP-MSI must conduct an information campaign on the protection/conservation of coastal resources and their value. In addition, if inventions are derived from the use of the materials, the collectors must provide training in a marine related discipline if there is a qualified candidate from the community.

Benefits realized to date: So far, only UP-MSI has received any substantial benefits through its close academic collaboration with the University of Utah. The Philippine government has received only negligible benefits in the short term, i.e. the annual bioprospecting fee (about US$ 200). Long-term benefits have not yet materialized, since none of the compounds isolated from the samples has yet been considered promising enough for international patenting and licensing.

Indirect benefits: The PIC procedure stipulated in EO 247 has been followed by the collectors, although it has not been easy to identify the local communities concerned in the case of marine resources. Nevertheless, with the help of NGO advisory services the communities have begun to exercise the rights they enjoy under EO 247. Furthermore, the consultation process has given communities the feeling that they are being taken seriously as users of regional marine biodiversity.

Direct contribution to poverty reduction

The direct contribution to poverty reduction is unpredictable because significant revenues will flow back to the Philippines only if a commercially successful product is developed from the materials collected. Furthermore, the benefits will depend on the result of the negotiations between the collectors and the party that commercializes the product. The CRA stipulates only that the Philippine government is to receive 5% of the revenues received by the collectors. How these revenues are channeled back to the indigenous or local community that originally granted the PIC has still to be defined.

Lessons learnt to date
This CRA is one of the few negotiated under EO 247, the first legislation anywhere in the world to implement Article 15 of the CBD on access and benefit-sharing at national level. The agreement provides for administrative fees to be paid to the Philippine government. Further benefits, which may flow back to indigenous and local communities or be used for conservation purposes in protected marine areas, can be generated only on the basis of patentable inventions that can be successfully commercialized. This focus in the benefit sharing agreement on successful commercialization is the weak point of the agreement, since in the short term only MSI profits from the close academic collaboration between the two institutions until a promising compound can be identified.

Case Study 5 The INBio-Merck agreement (*INBio*)

Type of genetic resource: Plants, insects and environmental samples to be evaluated for potential pharmaceutical and agricultural applications.

Actors involved
1) National Institute of Biodiversity of Costa Rica (INBio), a non-profit association established under Costa Rican law in 1989. INBio has a formal agreement with the Ministry of the Environment, allowing it to undertake specific activities relating to the national inventory and the utilization of the biodiversity in the protected areas.
2) Merck & Co., Inc.

How the genetic resource is used
A predetermined (confidential) number of processed plants, insects and environmental (micro-organism) samples are initially extracted and processed by INBio, and their pharmaceutical properties are explored at Merck facilities in Spain and the United States.

ABS agreement
The INBio-Merck agreement was signed in 1991, before the Convention on Biological Diversity was established, and renewed in 1994, 1996 and, for the last time, 1998.

Implementation and compliance instruments

A contract governed by Costa Rican law. Explicit compliance mechanisms entail only the payment of royalties. Article 3(d) states that, if an audit reveals an unfair payment in excess of 10%, the offending party must pay the full cost of the audit and correct the amount paid as soon as possible.

Benefits

Merck will provide INBio with a research fund of US$ 1million during the first two years of the agreement and contribute the laboratory equipment and materials needed by INBio to operate the laboratories for the processing of the samples at INBio and the University of Costa Rica. Merck will provide an additional fund to support INBio's work during any extension of the agreement. Merck agrees to pay royalties to INBio for any pharmaceutical product for human or animal use or for any product that can be used in agriculture that has been initially isolated or produced from any sample sent by INBio to Merck. The royalties will also apply to any product derived from or analogous to these compounds and to chemical compounds derived from living microorganisms isolated from environmental samples or from samples of dead tissue. The royalty percentage is considered to be confidential information and will not be divulged. It is within the range of percentages usually granted under this type of agreement. INBio will establish the necessary facilities in Costa Rica for the collection and processing of plants, insects and environmental samples. It will hire and train the personnel needed for the collection and processing of the samples. Merck agrees to provide training in its laboratories for INBio's personnel or whomever INBio appoints. The samples of plants and insects will be processed in a laboratory established by INBio at its own facilities and under a service subcontract at the University of Costa Rica.

Contributions and payments by INBIO's Bioprospecting Unit from 1991 to 2002, US$

91 - 93	94	95	96	97	98 - 2000	**Total**
100,040	43, 400	66, 670	51,092	95,196	242,057	**598, 455**
86,102	203,135	153,555	192,035	126,243	29,579	**790,649**
460,409	126,006	46,962	31,265	34,694	337,692	***1,037,028**
228,161	92,830	118,292	172,591	129,008	0	**740,882**
874,712	**465,371**	**385,479**	**446,983**	**385,141**	**609,328**	**3,167,014**

* Includes the value of INBio's equipment located at the University of Costa Rica

Source: INBio (2003)

Benefits realized to date: During the first two years of the agreement Merck paid INBio US$ 1 million in advance and provided an additional US$ 130,000 worth of laboratory equipment and material. Part of the money was allocated to the Costa Rican government's conservation programme, part was used by INBio for a complete inventory of the country's biological resources. No other information on the specific benefits of this agreement has been published. In the years after the trail-blazing Merck contract, INBio signed more agreements with other companies and scientific institutions. As of 2002, INBio's biodiversity prospecting agreements has generated almost US$ 600,000 for the Ministry, more than US$ 790,000 for Conservation areas and US$ 1,000,000 for public universities, as well as US$ 740,000 to cover INBio activities, particularly the national biodiversity inventory.

Indirect benefits: The agreement with Merck has triggered a number of cooperative projects involving INBio and other private sector companies and scientific institutions in the bioprospecting of Costa Rica's natural resources. A cooperation agreement signed in 1994 by INBio and the Ministry of the Environment and Energy governs INBio's responsibilities in the area of bioprospecting and specifies how it is to use the payments it receives. The agreement is valid for five years and is automatically renewed for the same period. It requires that the equivalent of at least 10% of the budget of each bioprospecting venture be used to support the management and protection of conservation areas and that 50% of any economic and material benefit (e.g. royalties) which INBio derives from the conclusion of bioprospecting contracts be transferred to the Ministry, which uses the money for the management and protection of conservation areas.

Direct contribution to poverty reduction

INBio has signed agreements not only with the industrial sector but also with the academic, non-governmental and governmental sectors. However, local communities have not yet shared in the economic benefits to any great extent. Men and women from the rural communities of Costa Rica, near protected areas, attend an intense, 6-month vocational course to become parataxonomists. The course covers the fundamentals of biology, ecology, taxonomy, evolution, collection and preservation techniques, techniques in data and information handling, equipment maintenance and administration, and everything that an individual has to know to combine individual fieldwork with teamwork. The employment of local residents is one of the direct benefits of conservation to the rural communities of the areas concerned. In addition to fieldwork and investigation, the parataxonomists disseminate their knowledge and impart the value of biodiversity to their own communities and parks through educational programmes aimed at their colleagues, neighbours, relatives and local schools.

Compared to other forest income activities in Costa Rica, such as forestry (which generates US$ 28 million p.a.) and tourism (US$ 421 million), the contribution made by the initial bioprospecting activities has been fairly small. However, a number of drugs are likely to be developed from Costa Rican genetic resources in the medium term. According to the World Resources Institute, even if INBio received only 2% of royalties on the sale of pharmaceuticals developed from Costa Rica's biodiversity, it would take "only" 20 drugs for INBio to be able to earn more funds than Costa Rica currently obtains from coffee and bananas, two of its major export crops.

Lessons learnt to date

The lack of transparency and information does not make it easy to evaluate the INBio-Merck agreement. Furthermore, the agreement does not provide for any measures to ensure the participation and compensation of all the stakeholders, especially the local and indigenous communities, or respect for their property rights. While not necessarily a model for other countries in itself, INBio is a very interesting example of how a particular bioprospecting effort – structured, designed and implemented before the CBD entered into force – has enabled a small biodiversity-rich country to enhance its national research capacities and establish a specific benefit-sharing arrangement that satisfies national interests. The INBio-Merck case is only one current institutional activity and is promoting further understanding of and research into Costa Rica's biodiversity, particularly in protected areas, where INBio undertakes the bulk of its activities. INBio's institutional policies are focused on adding value to national biodiversity by carrying out specialized research in the country and supplying potential academic and commercial users with information and initial products. In the case of the INBio-Merck deal not only are raw samples being supplied: they are also classified and pre-screened. Furthermore, passport information is coded in order to ensure that, if there should be any interest in future research and development processes, users are forced to return to INBio to obtain further materials or information.

In the above cases, traditional knowledge was involved in the *Kani, the Hoodia* and the *Kava cases*, but was not relevant in *INBio* and was not a specific focus in *MSI-Cancer*. It is important to observe that in these five cases two types of actors played a critical role in the ABS process. These are: (1) communities living in areas where genetic or biological resources could be cultivated or harvested; and (2) holders of traditional knowledge associated with genetic or biological resources. These actors are usually the most marginalized and disadvantaged. To strengthen these two categories of actors, the ABS regime needs to ensure that their knowledge is valued and safeguarded, and their participation is secured.

The experience demonstrated in the five case studies show that the benefits of ABS flow through different channels. In some cases, monetary benefit-sharing is based on expectations for the future ("blockbuster-hope"). In other cases, benefit-sharing occurs in the short term by providing income-generating job opportunities for locals. For some marginalized communities, the empowerment effect is more important than the monetary benefit. Yet in others, the provider countries focus on technology transfer and the build-up of a biotechnology industry. The five cases show a wide variety of benefits in both cash and kind: from funds for the communities involved (*Kani, Hoodia*) to potential or current employment opportunities (*Kani, Hoodia, Kava, INBio*); from the strengthening of the community's cultural identity and self-governance (*Kani, Hoodia*) to percentage-based options sometime in the future (*INBio, MSI-Cancer, Hoodia*), technology transfer and research cooperation, awareness creation and biodiversity inventories (*MSI-Cancer, INBio*).

The case studies provide major insights into how genetic resources and the sharing of the benefits arising from their use can contribute to poverty alleviation. The diverse benefit-sharing approaches revealed by the five case studies illustrate that ABS policies can contribute to creating opportunities for and empowerment of the poor.

Opportunities for the disadvantaged poor are promoted in a number of ways. At the most general level, ABS policies can foster economic growth, which in the long term could benefit the poor. From the five cases presented, *INBio* is most obviously pursuing this goal. It is the clear objective of *INBio* and its political supporters to increase the value added to genetic resources in Costa Rica. A similar idea can be identified in *Hoodia* and *MSICancer*, although the respective countries of origin seem to be pursuing a less stringent policy to achieve the goal. *Kani* and *Kava* are still at the stage where the region produces the raw material, while the value is added elsewhere. In the medium and long term, this strategy offers less prospect of economic growth since the suppliers of raw material are likely to lose market shares if more competitive substitute suppliers emerge or demand falls. On the other hand, *Kani*, *Kava* and, to some extent, *Hoodia* are promoting short-term opportunities for the local poor directly by providing employment opportunities. This is the most visible way for the local poor to share in the benefits derived from the use of their biological resources. It should be noted, however, that the local poor benefit by collecting or cultivating the biological resource. This approach to benefit-sharing is therefore similar to conventional trade in natural resources (e.g. timber). The difference from conventional trade lies in the genetic properties of the biological resources that are of interest to the user of the final product.

Opportunities for the poor could be promoted in the future through long-term benefit sharing. The *MSI-Cancer*, *INBio* and *Hoodia projects* included agreements on future benefit-sharing and represent cases of "blockbuster-hope". All the cases show that it is too early to assess the amount of monetary and non-monetary benefits that may accrue in the future. Consequently, it is not realistically possible to discuss the scale of the poverty-alleviating effect. But three important points are apparent. First, agreements relating to long term benefits-sharing increase the credibility of the bioprospecting project for the local communities as they are aware that they will share in any future profits. Second, funds seem to be an appropriate avenue for the distribution of monetary benefits in the region. Third, if local communities have only insecure benefits to look forward to (as in *MSI-Cancer* and *INBio*), an ABS arrangement is unlikely to materialize because for the local population, there is no beneficial monetary value of their biological resources.

As meager as the monetary benefits have hitherto been in the five case studies, they nevertheless point in the right direction. ABS agreements are used to transfer a certain amount of the present direct use value of genetic resources to the local poor. This is achieved primarily through the provision of employment opportunities. Long-term benefit-sharing is intended to transfer a share of the option value which the global gene fund has for humankind. Little has so far been achieved, but *INBio*, *MSI-Cancer* and *Hoodia* at least reveal the potential of ABS agreements in this respect. However, the *Kani* case also provides an example of how benefit-sharing may give rise to conflict even within an indigenous community. The agreements should therefore be drafted in a participatory process in order that they may take account of different perceptions within the local and indigenous communities and avoid treating them as a "black box".

Empowerment of the poor has been facilitated in some of the cases, most obviously in *Kani* and *Hoodia*. Both these cases provide potential turning points for indigenous communities from dependence on government welfare to self-governance. It has been the negotiation process rather than the benefits themselves that has catalyzed this process. Similarly, in *MSI-Cancer* it is the Prior Informed Consent process that has been instrumental in empowering the local and indigenous communities.

Benefits derived from the processes of distributing benefits as highlighted from the five case studies warrant a closer examination into the nature of participation in the sharing and distribution of benefits to be derived from Biodiversity.

Participation in Access and Benefit Sharing

The issue of ABS is closely linked to that of participation. Participation has been long recognized as an important link in delivering benefits of any development activity. The link between participation and the equitable sharing of benefits is strong in that the processes of participation are the same channels for ABS. The channels of ABS are established by creating forums of participation and strengthening the practices that allow the open channels of communication, for example if a benefit is education then the community that is to be educated must be receptive to the 'green' education that is to be disseminated by attending the workshop and positively using that knowledge. If participation is marginalized in that community, then a clear indication would be low levels of attendance at workshops and forums.

There is general consensus that participation is a key part of discussions about benefit sharing and that the fine tuning of the strategy of participation is the key issue to achieving equitable and fair benefit sharing. An important aspect of participation is the mutually strengthening relationship of benefit sharing such that the process of participation will distribute benefits (tangible and intangible) to participants involved in participation strategy cycle, thereby providing incentives to ensure the success of a project.

The increasing significance of participation as an approach to achieving successful projects has continued to strengthen because of the empirical evidence supporting this conviction. Participation is an approach which builds a process whereby a multidisciplinary approach is needed to handle the analysis of social, economic and environmental dimensions and their interactions. In the 1980s in realization to these needs, national strategies adopting a multidisciplinary approach were implemented with mixed success. As the experience of past strategies showed the more successful strategies appeared to be the more participatory. Conversely the less successful strategies appear to be the least participatory, therefore characterized by resilience to 'ownership' and 'commitment'.

Moreover, there are more general societal and foreign policy moves towards democracy and greater human rights, which appear to call for participation. Given the confusion over different meanings of participation, it is not surprising that there is great confusion between participation as a populist political movement and the more functional aspects of participation as applied to a strategy, irrespective of politics. Participation in such a strategy would clearly amount to a political process. It should be clear that the arguments for greater local-level empowerment, and the arguments for participation, have common roots and often the same protagonists, but they are not identical. This common misunderstanding occurs in PNG, where such an approach has been used as a political basis for building support to contest positions of leadership in parliament and lower levels of government.

In effect, a successful strategy is one in which capacity is built up to work and think strategically, as a product of all groups acting in concert. Strategy has been defined as comprising:

> A coordinated set of participatory and continuously improving processes of analysis, debate, capacity-strengthening, planning and investment, which integrates the economic, social and environmental objectives of society, seeking trade-offs where this is not possible.[26]

The need for the 'widest possible participation' in working towards a holistic strategy for sustainable development is noted in a number of chapters of Agenda 21 (Box 1), although there is little clarity about how to assure it. This is a tremendous challenge, without precedent. National laws and international conventions (such as the Aarhus Convention) have emerged to support a routine participatory approach in key decisions and actions.

---

[26] Dalal-Clayton (2002), p31.

Box 1. *Agenda 21 on Participation*

Agenda 21 refers to the need for broad participation in various chapters. For example:

In Chapter 8 (Integrating environment and development in decision-making): an adjustment or even a fundamental reshaping of decision-making, in the light of country specific conditions may be necessary if environment and development is to be put at the centre of economic and political decision-making, in effect achieving full integration of these factors.

In Chapter 23 (Strengthening the role of the major groups), Agenda 21 requires, in the specific context of environment and development, the need for new forms of participation and notes the need of individuals, groups and organizations to participate in decisions, particularly those which affect the communities in which they live and work.

In Chapter 26 (Recognizing and strengthening the role of indigenous people and their communities), active participation is called for to incorporate their 'values, views and knowledge'.

In Chapter 33 (Financial resources and mechanisms): priorities should be established by means that incorporate public participation and community involvement providing equal opportunity for men and women … In this respect, consultative groups and round tables and other nationally-based mechanisms can play a facilitative role.

In Chapter 37 (National mechanisms and international cooperation for capacity-building): as an important aspect of overall planning, each country should seek internal consensus at all levels of society on policies and programmes needed for short- and long-term capacity building to implement its Agenda 21 programme. This consensus should result from a participatory dialogue of relevant interest groups and lead to an identification of skill gaps, institutional capacities and capabilities, technological and scientific requirements and resource needs to enhance environmental knowledge and administration to integrate environment and development.

Source: UNCED 1992

Although Agenda 21 calls for participation in all elements of the strategy cycle it is also important to understand that there are implications of participation for the political status quo in any given context.

The framework proposal for the ABS should be neither be prescriptive nor focus solely on projects. Rather a certain amount of flexibility is crucial for ensuring effective benefit sharing and enabling various stakeholders (in the process of their participation) determine benefit sharing details.

There are the key constraints preventing the participation cycle from distributing the positive outcomes of benefit sharing. One such effect is that constraints may occur as result of beneficiaries' unrealistic expectations being unfulfilled about the length of time in which participation can yield results in practice and policies. However it is important that at the beginning and throughout the life of the project, indicators (both quantitative and qualitative) of benefit sharing should be developed in consultation with all stakeholders to be used as tools for monitoring the levels of benefit sharing and evaluating the parallel impact of benefits on beneficiaries.

There are clearly some costs of participation. From the outset, extensive participation is very costly and unrealistic because in some situations, participation may cause reactions that are not necessarily helpful for the participatory approach. In fact, may be a negating effect on the participatory approach in that a complete consensus is an impossibility, rather an agreement of compromise encourages ownership of the process.

The Nature of Benefit Sharing in PNG

There are some indications that PNG that it is beginning to take positive steps toward Access and Benefit Sharing. The current initiative also indicates that stakeholders are interested in pursuing ABS as a development tool to reshape the existing benefits-sharing models to ensure development benefits are shared equitably amongst increasing number of Papua New Guineans.

Changing the ABS paradigm in PNG will at first be difficulty because of existing practices particularly in the natural resource sector which promotes the marginalization and exclusion of many stakeholders in the development processes. The benefit-sharing practices in the fisheries, forestry and mining sectors will be reviewed to assist the government in formulating an appropriate ABS regime. In the mining sector the Ok Tedi Mining Project will be assessed because of its advanced benefit sharing framework.

Fisheries Sector

The fisheries sector is important to the livelihood of the coastal communities in PNG. The ABS regime that exists is basically confined to a two party – the State and the fishing company process. The State benefits through revenue collected from access fees, licensing fees and taxes. The fishing company benefits through accessing the fisheries resources of the country and profits from the sale of the fisheries resources. Gaining any meaningful insight from this process is limited because of the nature of the arrangement (confidential) and the limited number of actors in the process.

Following a review of the sector[27], several lessons which are relevant for the present purpose can be identified. These are:

- projects should not be stand alone but either be part of a bigger programme or be appropriately linked and integrated with other programs so that benefits can be gained through the sharing of information, experience and other values generated by collaborative approach;
- a cost-benefit analysis assessing all facets of the project should be undertaken, before the project proceeds;
- projects should be simple and robust, utilising available skills and appropriate technology;
- stakeholders should be closely involved in fishery projects - from feasibility to the operational phase;
- training in previous artisanal fishing projects was absent. All fishery projects should include a training component;
- implementation schedules should be realistic with close monitoring; and
- government should integrate and create more avenues for subsistence fishermen to participate in the cash economy, thereby building up the skills, knowledge and experience for them to move into artisanal fishing.

These are important considerations which must be taken into account in designing an appropriate ABS framework. A crucial gap in the fisheries sector is the lack of participation by local communities in the decision making process. A transparent and inclusive participatory process promotes good governance and strengthens and empowers local people.

Forestry Sector

The forestry sector approaches ABS with a two-edged sword. On the one hand, the forestry law and policy encourage and promote the active participation of resource owners in the development of their forestry resources. The regulatory system enables the involvement of the resources at the initial stages of resources allocation (forest management agreement) to the engagement of a logging company in the project (logging permit). On the other hand, it falls short of providing transparent mechanisms for the supervision and monitoring of the relationship between loggers and the resource owners.

As soon as access is obtained by the State, forest resource owners are left to fend for themselves with the logger with very little or no government controls. The forest resource owners and the loggers negotiate the terms and

[27] Rural Coastal Fisheries Development Project (2003) (Draft) (Unpublished)

conditions of the logging project in an agreement called the Logging and Marketing Agreement. The Logging and Marketing Agreement sets out the types of benefits to be shared between the two parties. The government benefits through the permits process and the revenue from logging taxation.

As the Logging and Marketing Agreement are confidential commercial agreements and are therefore not subject to public scrutiny. In 1998 a comprehensive review of the forestry sector and the benefits of logging projects obtained by the different parties was conducted by Colin Filer who found that:

- Most landowner companies having been formed for the exclusive purpose of 'capturing' a foreign logging contractor, within a space which had been cleared by the failure of previous experiments in rural development and for which traditional models of collective enterprise were clearly inadequate.
- Representatives encouraged to perform several tasks or functions which serve social rather than commercial aims of resource owners such as:
  (1) negotiate the basic conditions of project development, especially the priorities for social and economic infrastructure,
  (2) formulating and applying rules for the distribution of project revenues earmarked for the benefit of the entire community,
  (3) lobbying for greater community access to project employment or business development opportunities, and
  (4) organizing activities designed to promote the regeneration of forests which have already been logged.
- The demand for resource development is undermining indigenous models of community leadership even at the community level where clans, like landowner companies, are now presenting themselves as the recipients and redistributors of resource rents.
- Developers have one great advantage, that the people in the centre of the operations, with the greatest power to shut them down, also have the strongest claim to compensation for their lost resources.
- The long-term approach of a project to establishing stakeholder committees is definitely better than rapid reconnaissance missions.
- The local 'business' ventures fail to meet community expectations, or else become a new focus of factional dispute within the community, because Western business management methods remain fundamentally incompatible with the 'Melanesian way' of redistributing material wealth.
- Landowning communities manifest a common desire for more information about costs and benefits of different conservation and development options. [28]

There is confusion of failed expectations, lack of information and awareness about the details of projects, lack of understanding are contributing factors to

[28] Filer, C (1998)

the failures of projects. The purpose of participation is not for the purpose of involving stakeholders rather there are a series of opportunistic moves to legitimize project operations. Generally there is overall dissatisfaction over the sharing and distribution of benefits in the forestry sector.

Two of the issues which need to be addressed by an ABS framework are: how have changes in the distribution of wealth, power and knowledge between resource owners and other stakeholders affected the way that resource owners think about their development choices? And why do landowner communities in different parts of the country make different choices on development?

Mining Sector

The mining sector has over the years developed a comprehensive framework for benefit sharing. The reason being that monetary benefits from mining projects far outweighs those of the other sectors. Table 4 shows the types of benefits that are shared amongst the different stakeholders in the mining sector. Mining projects have fueled economic growth in the country and enabled the opening up of the country through infrastructure and physical development in mining project areas and the provinces. In fact the mining sector contributes more than 70 percent of revenue to the national pursue.

Table 4: *Benefits in Mining Projects*[29]

Who benefits? **Stakeholders**	**Name of Benefit**	**What are the benefits?** **Tangible**	 **Intangible**	**How are the benefits distributed?**
National Government				
Provincial Government	1. Special Support Grant - Duration of active project phase 2. Royalty Distribution 3. Equity 4. Preference in Training Employment and Business 5. OLLPG	Calculated at 1% of fob 80% Levies in the form of i) infrastructural development levies; and ii) economic development - land use follow-up levies; and iii) community and social development	Grant tied to expenditure on specific projects (minimum % within project area) Priority given to people from provinces	Annual grant paid to the Provincial Government by the National Government

[29] The Table is incomplete because of lack of available information at the time of data compilation.

		levies; and iv) any other levies as are from time to time determined by national law or by agreement		
Local Level Government				
Resource Owners	1. Royalty Distribution 2.Tripartite Agreement 3. Equity 4. Preference in Training, Employment and Business 5. Direct Assistance for the Formation of a L/owner Company/Business Development	- 5% as cash to landowners - 10% to the children and future generations of landowners - occupational fees at K5 per hectare to landowners - a fee for restricted access, commencing at K2.50/ha/annum, and inc to K7.50/ha/annum by the third yr of the lease - a payment to the non-renewable resource fund, held in trust for l/owners at 5/ha/annum - fees cleared for land at K5/ha/annum National Government provides direct assistance for the formation in the form of an outright loan, K500 000 or a loan guarantee.	Priority be given to landowners.	
Clan	1. Preference in Training Employment and Business		Priority be given to people from mining areas	
Village	1. Royalty Distribution	5% on community projects determined by landowners		
Resource Developer	?	?		
Researcher/ Scientist	?	?		
Institution	?	?		

Source: Mawuli (2000)

However, health, education and other such development indicators illustrate that the benefits to the mining communities are usually short term, leaving the communities "poorer". Socio-economic baseline surveys conducted in some of the mining projects reveal extensive environmental damage, low economic activity in the local area, high dependence on external sources of income generation, communities experiencing health issues directly related to the mine activities and finally dissatisfaction about the benefits received from the mine operations. The percentages of benefits received by the different stakeholders particularly the resource owners usually yield unsustainable results.

In the case of the Ok Tedi Mining Project, a study conducted in 2000 clearly showed that the benefits paid to the government authorities or clans for distribution are not reaching all the potential beneficiaries.[30] The challenge here is identifying and maintaining relationships that will allow the channels of communication and the accessing of benefits to be maintained throughout the lifespan of a project. It would seem then that stakeholders need to operate separately in order to be firm in receiving benefits and not be dependant on the administration of another stakeholder, thereby allowing duplicity to occur.

The different approaches to benefit-sharing adopted by these three sectors show that ABS is pragmatic in PNG. Benefit sharing in the fisheries sector is exclusive in nature, while the forestry sector illustrates the complex nature of participation in PNG. In the mining sector the current framework has not yielded a fair and equitable sharing of benefits.

In principle then PNG adopts and supports ideas that exhibit a semblance of the concept of ABS but in reality, benefit sharing is difficult to implement successfully. This situation can be attributed to the lack of a national ABS framework in the country.

Summary

Benefit sharing in PNG is critical to ensuring that Papua New Guineans benefit (both tangible and intangible) from the management of their biological resources. It is therefore imperative that benefit sharing should not be based on the assumption that beneficiaries should become "rich". A national ABS framework must essentially lead to equitable and fair outcomes for all the parties and also the elimination of the inequalities inherent in the current practices.

---

[30] Middle Fly Socio-Economic Baseline Survey (2000) and Kiunga-Tabubil Highway Socio-Economic
Baseline Survey (2000) (both unpublished)

There are several important principles that must be applied to guide the formulation of an ABS framework. These include:

- equity and fairness[31];
- application of a participation strategy that needs to be relevant to the context, specific to that area of application, and importantly there are checks and balances in place to govern that the benefit sharing framework; and
- integrate people-centered development which is crucial to the process and overall success of benefit sharing regime.[32]

The real challenge of a successful ABS is to deliver goods and services through relationships which are strengthened over time. The primary concern always hinges on what has been delivered, and not on how the goods and services were delivered. The key value that drives benefit-sharing is the conscious decision to ensure that benefits are shared through a participation strategy that is *inclusive* rather than exclusive of all beneficiaries throughout the lifespan of the project, from planning and research to commercialization. Participation in the benefit sharing process begins as one party depends on another, but as the process develops over time, power shifts within the stakeholders themselves such that during the commercialization stage, the power rests with stakeholders completely removed from the natural environment. The challenge is to ensure that *despite changing dynamics in relationships between stakeholders*, benefits should continue to be shared fairly and equitably.

[31] *Equitable* – all beneficiaries receive benefits that allows them to gain in such a way that benefits are not widening the gap between the haves and have nots; and *Fair* – all beneficiaries receive benefits in manner that is fair.

[32] The two main concerns that should be included are: (1) the involvement (and rights) of the holders of traditional knowledge; and (2) provision must be made in the benefit-sharing regime for the alleviation of the poverty of the local population to be one of the criteria for the benefits to be agreed. If by the end of the project the levels of poverty in the immediate area has increased or human development has not improved then it can be rightly stated that benefit sharing in that area has failed.

Chapter 5. National Policies and their Impact on ABS

Dr. Eric Kwa and Dr. Alphonse Gelu

Introduction

Papua New Guinea is a unique country as it is blessed with vast natural resources and natural beauty. Before contact was made with outsiders over 100 years ago, people lived off these resources for thousands of years. Since contact with the outside world and the establishment of formal government in PNG, the people of PNG have been exposed to many outside influences some of which have had adverse impacts on the country and its natural resources and the environment. Natural resources have taken on a new face - a source of economic benefits for development for the people and the government. Natural resources have thus become the 'milking cow' for the government, people and the industry.

Traditionally, PNG was depicted by different development theorist as comprising traditional institutional structures and activities. These structures and activities define the different types of relationships that exist between the people and their environment. This means that the resources that are found in the country are collectively owned by the people. This form of ownership defines the relationships that exist between the different groups of people in a village or a specific area as well as the relationship the people have towards the land. It is therefore a requirement that the ownership of the land must be clearly established in order to allow the owners to benefit from whatever development that is taking place with regard to the use of the land or the exploitation of the natural resources that is found on the land.

One of the purposes of this Chapter is to review existing and proposed national policies and ascertain how they relate to ABS. The policies that are covered include those that are closely related to the environment and the sustainable use of resources. These policies will be considered from the perspective of the government and other groups that are concerned with the sustainable use of resources in the country. The current government of Sir Michael Somare has placed emphasize on the environment and its use for future generations. This is indicated in his call for the 'Coalition of

Rainforest Nations' in Japan in 2005. The government's commitment to protecting the environment is also stated in the MTDS 2005–2010. This aspect of the MTDS will be further discussed in the Chapter as part of the government's policy towards environmental protection.

The country faces a dilemma between economic growth through the exploitation of natural resources and sustainable development. The issue of sustainable development is now an important element in the exploitation of natural resources in the country. It is therefore the responsibility of the government adopt a regulatory regime that promotes the sustainable use of the country's natural resources.

Policy is the aspect of politics which concerns most people. Policy consists of the outputs of the political process. It reflects the impact of government on society, that is, its ability to make things better or to make things worse. The field of political analysis which developed in the 1960s and 1970s does not deal only with issues of efficiency and effectiveness with 'how of policy making' but also addresses the 'what of policy making', that is the nature of government outputs and their outcomes for the larger society.

What is a Policy?

A policy, in a general sense according to Heywood:

> ... is a plan of action adopted by, for example, an individual, group, business or government. To designate something as a policy implies that a formal decision has been made, giving official sanction to a particular course of action. Public policy can therefore be seen as the formal or stated decisions of government bodies. However, policy is better understood as the linkage between intentions, actions and results. At the level of *intentions*, policy is reflected in the stance of government (what government says it will do). At the level of *actions*, policy is reflected in the behaviour of government (what government actually does). At the level of *results*, policy is reflected in the consequences of government action (the impact of government on the larger society) (1997, p. 382).

The policy process relates to the mechanisms through which public (government) policy is made. Policy making comes in two processes. Firstly, it involves a linked series of actions and events. This starts off with the throwing of ideas around, debate on the ideas and analysis and evaluation and finally the making of a formal decision for implementation. The second process distinguishes the 'how' of government from the 'what' of government. It focuses on the way in which policy is made (process), rather than on the substance of policy itself and its consequences.

Policy is also an output of a political process. According to American Political Scientist David Easton (1953), this was exactly what he saw and included in his model of a modern political system. The policy process in the system by Easton is seen in what comes out from the government which forms the output of the system. The output comprises the different approaches that governments take relating to a particular issue or issues. The approaches, thus comes in the form of policies because their main intention is to address problems that have been identified.

Policy according to another well known scholar Aaron Wildavsky (1979) is a process as well as a product. It is a process because it goes through a screening system before it can be fully realized and it is a product because it goes through a process and what is achieved is the policy. The making and implementation of a policy or policies follows a well defined process (Hague and Harrop, 1987, 298). The process is:

1. Initiation - the decision to make a decision in a particular area; otherwise known as agenda-setting
2. Formulation - the detailed development of a policy into concrete proposals
3. Implementation - putting the policy into practice
4. Evaluation - appraising the consequences and success of the policy

Two famous models of policy analysis are offered in the synoptic (Simon, 1983) and incremental (Lindblom, 1979) models. There is a general agreement that most governments follow the incremental model of policy analysis although some aspects of the synoptic model are used in order to improve the quality of policy making. According to Hague and Harrop (1987), the synoptic model requires decision-makers to examine a problem in a comprehensive way. Specifically policy-makers must:

1. rank all their values;
2. formulate clear options;
3. calculate all the results for choosing each option; and
4. select the alternative which achieves most values.

The model requires a comprehensive approach in dealing with the issues. However, policy-makers usually apply the process of bounded rationality to make policy making more manageable. This eliminates the comprehensiveness required by the model (Hague and Harrop, 1987). As a result, decision makers focus on a few 'good looking' options and look only for a satisfactory rather than the best solution.

The incremental model on the other hand involves change by small steps. According to Hague and Harrop (1987), its central feature is that policy is continually made and re-made in a series of small adjustments rather than as a result of a single, comprehensive analysis. It represents what Lindblom calls the 'science of muddling through', an approach which may not lead to the achievement of grand objectives but which at least avoids the making of huge mistakes. In incremental policy-making what matters is not that those involved should agree on objectives but that agreement should be reached on the desirability of following a particular policy even when basic objectives differ. Policy emerges from rather than precedes negotiation with interested groups.

A general review of the policies which have an impact on biodiversity reveals that PNG uses the incremental model, particularly in relation policies relating to the forestry, fishing, and mining sectors. This is also evident in the overall objectives of government development plans such as the MTDS and the policies on the environment. For the present purpose, the synoptic model is relevant for the formulation of an ABS framework. The reason being that decision-makers should try and consider all the consequences of the relevant options for all values before reaching a conclusion on how best they would approach the issue of ABS. However, once a policy is in place as a result of appropriate deliberations, then the incremental model would become relevant because it would allow decision-makers to make small adjustments to patch up any defects. The defects should be those that are being experienced and not what is envisioned for the future even though considering the future is an important consideration.

A crucial factor that must be considered at the very beginning is the capacity of governments to formulate and implement policies pertaining to biodiversity. PNG is known for lacking the capacity to formulate relevant policies and successfully implementing them over sustained periods. The proposed ABS framework considered in this paper must be fully supported by the government to ensure its success in the long term. The government should not pay lip-service to such an important policy. The lack of capacity of governments is now evident in the implementation of the current MTDS[33]. The lack of government capacity can affect the required direction in which a policy is supposed to address. The danger here is that policies relating to biodiversity in PNG would end up in a similar manner. However, if there is real commitment by the various stakeholders which includes the government, then the policies would achieve their intended objectives.

Shaping National Development through the National Goals and Directive Principles and the MTDS

An examination of different government policies of the last 30 years reveals that the government has not been able to follow any credible and tangible development path. The piecemeal approach to national development may be attributed to, among other factors, institutional and human incapacities and

[33] Satish Chand stated recently that "Papua New Guinea's Medium Term Development Strategy (MTDS) has not delivered on its intent", *The National*, June 5th 2006. A recent study by Yala, Mawuli and Sanida also confirms this view. See Yala, C, Mawuli, A and Sanida, O., The Medium Term Development Strategy 2005-2010 (Port Moresby: NRI, 2006)

political instability. The only significant attempt that has been made by the government which had any semblance of a national development vision is the five yearly MTDS. The last MTDS (1997-2002) was described as a failure. The current MTDS will head in the same direction if remedial measures are not taken to arrest its defects.

In this section of the Chapter several major policies will be reviewed in some detail to ascertain their focus on biodiversity and the sustainable use of biological resources. The aim of the exercise is to establish the linkage between these polices and biodiversity conservation and sustainable use so that the formulation of the ABS framework will be able to positively contribute to the attainment of these major government policies.

The National Goals and Directive Principles

When PNG became an independent State in 1975, it adopted and declared its *Constitution* as the supreme law of the land. This stipulation is expressly stated by section 10 and 11 of the *Constitution*. The *Constitution* has therefore, become the guiding principle of the country over the last 29 years. In the Preamble of the *Constitution* are the country's development visions. These development goals are called the "National Goals and Directive Principles" (NGDP). The NGDP focuses its attention on all the different facets of economic, social and political development. There are five National Goals and supporting Directive Principles. These are:

1. Integral Human Development;
2. Equality and Participation;
3. National Sovereignty and Self Reliance;
4. Natural Resources and the Environment; and
5. Papua New Guinean Ways.

The NGDP serve as the foundation for any government development plan. All national plans, whether short or long-term, must aim to: (1) achieve the full human development of every Papua New Guinean; (2) provide equal opportunities for the participation of every Papua New Guinean in the development process; (3) promote national identity and enable Papua New Guineans to be economically and politically self reliant; (4) promote sustainable use of the country's natural resources and enhance the carrying capacity of the natural environment; and (5) promote Papua New Guinean ways.

As in other countries, both in the West and the Third World, the Constitutional Planning Committee (CPC) in its deliberations was looking for a set of guidelines that would act as the anchor for development then and in the future. Any policy dealing with development should be considered according to the different principles of the NGDP. Anything outside of this would be deemed inappropriate. This is because the drawing of the NGDP was based on what King, Lee and Waraka (1985) as "homegrown fruit of grass-roots consultation and prolonged deliberation by the CPC".

The NGDP is a plan or blue print for the government and the people of PNG as a whole. The NGDP reflect the aspirations of past, present and future Papua New Guineans. The NGDP is PNG's road-map to prosperity and happiness[34].

The NGDP have been amplified in various government policies since Independence. All the present national development plans attribute their very existence to NGDPS. Bold statements are usually expressed in the introductory part of a national development plan declaring that the policy is aimed at achieving the National Goals.

The Medium Term Development Strategy 2005-2010

Since independence, successive governments have introduced their development programs to improve the livelihood of the people of PNG. In the 1990s the government began to adopt rolling five year development program. The last five year development program was the MTDS 1997 – 2002. The primary vision of that MTDS was to build a partnership between the government and the people.

> The vision of the MTDS is of Government, the community of the one Nation, working with local communities that together make up the Nation. Where a community is pooling resources to build and run a school or an aid post, the Government can help out by providing a teacher or a community health worker.

In the five years since its inception in 1997, the MTDS did not provide the impetus for rural growth and sustainable development of the country. The ending of the MTDS 1997-2002 also coincided with the election of a new government in 2002. With a new government in power, the policies and strategies of a previous government are bound to be changed. Against this backdrop the Government of Michael Somare has embarked on a policy shift focusing on three broad areas. These are:

- Good Governance;
- Export-driven Economic Growth; and
- Rural Development, Poverty Reduction and Human Resource Development.

The third objective may be split into three separate policy objectives – rural development; poverty reduction and human resource development. The three broad areas have been further cemented in the 2005 – 2010 MTDS. The 2005 – 2010 MTDS has ten guiding principles. They are:

[34] Kwa, EL., *Papua New Guinea Constitutional Law* (Sydney: Law Book Co, 2001)

1. Private Sector-led Economic Growth
2. Resource Mobilisation and Alignment
3. Improvements in the Quality of Life
4. Natural Endowments
5. Competitive Advantage and the Global Market
6. Integrating the Three Tiers of Government
7. Partnership Through Strategic Alliances
8. Least Developed Access Intervention
9. Empowering Papua New Guineans and Improving Skills
10. 'Sweat Equity and Papua New Guinean Character

Like in the previous MTDS, the main development strategy is defined as export-driven economic growth, rural development and poverty reduction, including good governance and the promotion of agriculture, forestry, fisheries and tourism on a sustainable basis. This strategy is said to be realized by empowering Papua New Guineans, especially those in rural areas, to mobilize their own resources for higher living standards.

Under the economic growth strategy of the MTDS, focus is placed on areas that would certainly have an effect on biodiversity and environment protection. These areas include the primary sector which comprise of agriculture, forestry and fisheries, tourism, mining, petroleum and gas and finally manufacturing and downstream processing. These are all resources driven activities which would involve the exploitation of the natural resources and the relationships that the people especially those in rural areas have. There are clear indications that despite the emphasis given to these resources sectors, the government is committed towards the protection of the environment. In the MTDS the government has made it clear that:

> Protection of the natural environment is also a constitutional obligation and is captured by the fourth National Goal and Directive Principle of Natural Resources and Environment. Ecologically sustainable development is a necessary condition to ensure that PNG's development policies are sustainable over the long term, and it is an explicit objective under the MTDS.[35]

Table 6.1 of the MTDS shows the National Goals and Targets. There are seven goals all together:

1. Eradicate Extreme Poverty and Hunger
2. Achieve Universal Primary Education
3. Promote Gender Equality and Empower Women
4. To Reduce Child Mortality

---

[35] PNG Government., The Medium Term Development Strategy: Our Plan for Economic and Social Advancement (Port Moresby: 2005) 44.

5. To Improve Maternal Health
6. Combat HIV/AIDS, Malaria and Other Diseases
7. Ensure Environment Sustainability

The target and the different indicators of goal seven as appears in Table 6.1 can be shown as Table 5 below. This goal is specific on the forecast of sustainable development in the next five to ten years. The indicators of the targets include areas of forestry, protection of biological diversity including land and marine areas, protection of biodiversity in mining areas as well as the effects of energy resources on the environment and most importantly the emissions of carbon dioxide which would have an adverse effect on the environment.

It is therefore important for the government to put in place policies that would absorb each of these target areas and identify specific locations in which these policies would apply. It is imperative that the policies must take into consideration the sustainable use of the different resources that are identified. For example, in the case for re-forestation, the current policy dealing with re-forestation must apply to areas identified and there must be in place a process dealing with the sustainable use of the forest before any logging may take place. Similar considerations must apply to other resource activities.

Table 5: *Goal Seven – Ensure Environmental Sustainability: Targets and Indicators*

GOAL 7 **ENSURE ENVIRONMENTAL SUSTAINABILITY**	
Target 12 Implement the principles of sustainable development through sector specific programs by 2010 and no later than 2015	**Indicators** 40. Percentage of land area covered by primary forest 41. Primary forest depletion rate (percentage) per year 42. Re-forestation rate (percentage) per year 43. Percentage of land area protected to maintain biological diversity 44. Percentage of marine area protected to maintain biological diversity 45. Percentage land rehabilitated to ensure biodiversity (mines) 46. GDP per unit of energy use (as proxy for energy efficiency) 47. Carbon dioxide emissions (per capita)
Target 13 By 2020, increase commercial use	48. Percentage land used for commercial purposes

of land and natural resources through improvements in environmentally friendly technologies and methods of protection	49. Percentage of cultivable land used for agricultural production 50. Agricultural exports as a percentage of all exports 51. Value of agricultural exports as a percent of total GDP 52. Value of non-agriculture exports as percent of GDP 53. Percentage of commercial operations using sustainable practices

Source: MTDS 2005 - 2010

The real challenge for the government is to make this development program work. A key concern about the MTDS is that is does not provide a clear nexus between the priorities identified by the MTDS and sustainable development. The MTDS makes a brisk mention of sustainable development and ties it loosely with forestry and fisheries resources development, but it fails to clearly provide the strategy to achieve sustainable development, not only in these two sectors, but also on a national level.

Policies on Aspects of Biodiversity

There is currently no specific national policy on biodiversity. The policy that comes closest to biodiversity protection and sustainable use is the Environment Policy of 1976. However, this policy is quite broad and does not itself focus directly on biodiversity protection and sustainable use. Several national policies also have some bearing on aspects of biological diversity. These include forestry, fisheries, agriculture, transport and tourism. Each of the policies governing these sectors and their relationship to biodiversity protection and sustainable use are examined to provide some guide in the formulation of the proposed ABS framework.

Environment Policy

The government has since Independence in 1975, recognized the value of this unique biodiversity and made provision for its protection, sustainable use and management. The *Constitution* of PNG expressly calls for the protection, wise use and replenishment of the country's biodiversity and natural resources. This is set out in Goal 4 of the *Constitution*. Goal 4 is in the following terms:

> We declare our fourth goal to be for Papua New Guinea's natural resources and environment to be conserved and used for the collective benefit of us all, and be replenished for the benefit of future generations.
>
> WE ACCORDINGLY CALL FOR—
>
> (1) wise use to be made of our natural resources and the environment in and on the land or seabed, in the sea, under the land, and in the

air, in the interests of our development and in trust for future generations; and

(2) the conservation and replenishment, for the benefit of ourselves and posterity, of the environment and its sacred, scenic, and historical qualities; and

(3) all necessary steps to be taken to give adequate protection to our valued birds, animals, fish, insects, plants and trees.

This constitutional mandate was supplemented in 1976, with the introduction of the national environmental policy. The environmental policy entitled "Environment and Conservation Policy: A Statement of Principles" among other things, seeks to foster proper environmental management for the benefit of the present and future generations and the consideration of biodiversity protection and sustainable use in economic planning. The Environment Policy merely restates and expands the fourth Goal of the National Goals and Directive Principles. Five key principles are articulated by the environment policy. These are:

1. Development must be economical, social and ecological;
2. Wise use of non-renewable natural resources;
3. Recognition of the ability of the environment to produce renewable resources;
4. Safeguarding and wisely managing the wildlife and their habitat in the development process; and
5. Planning to be applied to human settlement and urbanisation.

This policy framework does clearly accommodate biological diversity protection and sustainable use. The policy recognizes the important link between social and economic progress and their impact on biodiversity.

An important aspect of the policy is that it shifts the responsibility for ensuring the maintenance of biological diversity from the national government (acting alone) to individuals, families, clans and local-level governments.[36] It is therefore, imperative to understand that the government and every Papua New Guinean, old and young, male and female, big and small alike are all required to act, as custodians of the country's biological resources. The onus is thus, on every one to ensure that development activities do not adversely affect the country's rich and unique biodiversity.

The underpinning of the Environment Policy is that biodiversity protection and its sustainable use must be given consideration in planning for economic development. This Environment Policy provided the foundation for environment and resources use and planning since 1976.

The main setback of the Environment Policy is that it does not provide strategies to achieve the integration of sustainable development in national

[36] Kwa, EL., Country Report (1998) 3 *Asia Pacific Environmental Law Journal* 333

programs for economic and social development. This weakness has resulted in past and present national policies paying lip service to the environment policy. The Environment Policy has remained unchanged for 31 years. Some of the modern principles of environmental management such as, inter-generational equity; intra-generational equity and integration clearly fall outside the scope of the Environment Policy. There is a strong case for a revision of the Environment Policy to enable it to mirror the values and aspirations of a contemporary PNG society.

Forest Policy

The forestry sector has undergone major policy and legislative changes since the early 1990s. A new forestry policy was introduced in 1990 on the back of the World Bank report into the forestry sector (Tropical Forest Action Plan 1986) and the infamous Barnett Commission of Inquiry in 1987. The National Forest Policy 1990 is aimed at streamlining and strengthening access to forestry resources and their utilization and removing corruption in the sector. The Forest Policy seeks to address these objectives through a series of strategies. These include: (1) Forest Management; (2) Forest Industry; (3) Forest Research; (4) Forestry Training and Education and (5) Forestry Organisation and Administration. These essential components of the National Forest Policy are designed to enhance the forestry sector and transform it into a viable sector. Each of these components is critical to the forestry sector.

Forestry management involves issues of resource ownership, classification and resources acquisition. Rules relating to access to the forestry resources are located in this part of the policy. The primary tool for access is the Forest Management Agreement. Unfortunately, the policy does not contain clear rules about PIC and benefit sharing. The actual benefit sharing arrangements are left to the vices of the developers and the forest resource owners through the Logging and Marketing Agreements with very little supervision by the National Forest Authority.

Forest research is promoted through the auspices of the National Forest Research Institute which is based in Lae. Again the Forest Policy does not provide clear directives as to access to forestry resources and PIC for research, and benefit sharing in relation to research results.

The draft Eco-Forestry Policy which was promulgated in 2003 also does not clarify issues relating to access to forestry genetic resources and potential benefit sharing. The draft policy seeks to complement the National Forest Policy by strengthening the management and protection of the country's forest resources through the regulation of eco-forestry activities.

A key proposal of the draft policy which has potential impacts on ABS is biodiversity inventory. Under the draft policy, it is proposed that a national biodiversity inventory will be undertaken jointly by several government institutions (including universities) and non-governmental organisations. The inventory will cover all forestry resources including flora and fauna species. This national database will be updated every 20 years. The policy promotes institutional collaboration and seeks to strengthen institutional networking.

Another crucial aspect of the draft policy is biodiversity conservation. Under the draft policy, the National Forest Authority will establish a network of conservation areas throughout the country. Where an area has been declared a conservation forest area, it is proposed that all commercial activities that by their nature would jeopardize the functions of the forest ecosystems will be banned.

These two components of the draft Eco-Forestry Policy will have a direct bearing on ABS. However, the draft policy provides very little guidance as to how the government intends to obtain PIC from resource owners in relation to conservation areas and also, the kinds of costs and benefits that will be derived through biodiversity conservation and biodiversity inventory.

Fisheries Policy

A comprehensive fisheries sector review was undertaken in the early 1990s. The review was funded largely by external donors, primarily the Asian Development Bank, AusAid and the Food and Agriculture Organisation. The review resulted in the introduction of a major fisheries policy and a legislative enactment in 1993. These changes also saw the birth of the National Fisheries Authority which replaced the Department of Fisheries and Marine Resources. The restructuring of the National Fisheries Authority as a statutory authority was completed in 1999.

The primary focus of the fisheries sector reform is the sustainable use and management of commercial fisheries resources. The narrow focus of the fisheries sector on commercial fishing activities limits its impact on generic marine biological resources.

One of the visions of the National Fisheries Authority is to develop, promote and strengthen its relationship with provincial governments because it believes that fostering a cordial relationship with the provinces will lead to the sustainable use and management of the country's fisheries resources. In addressing this issue and also to ensure clear demarcation of powers, roles and responsibilities between the two levels of government, the National Fisheries Authority has embarked on a plan to engage the participation of Maritime Provinces in fisheries management through agreements in the form of memorandums of understanding. Several memorandums of understanding have been executed between the National Fisheries Authority and some of the maritime provinces.

The limited focus of the fisheries policy and law means that local-level governments and to some limited extent the provincial governments can develop their own generic marine resources law and policy to regulate marine biological resources in their areas of administration. In this regard, some of the provinces, such as Manus, Morobe and East Sepik have proceeded to develop their own provincial fishery laws. Three local-level government, namely, the Talasea, Hoskins and Bialla Rural Local-level Governments have also enacted their local marine environment laws pursuant to s44 of the OLPGLLG to regulate access, sustainable use and management of its marine biological resources. These provincial and local laws have to be taken into account when developing the ABS framework.

Agriculture Policy

More than 85% of Papua New Guineans live in the rural areas of the country. These people live off their land, producing mostly subsistence crops. The main source of income for these rural dwellers is agricultural cash crops. Agriculture therefore, plays a pivotal role in the lives of these rural people and the national economy. Given its importance to the people and the economy, successive governments have over the years tried to concentrate their efforts in this sector through the introduction of several agricultural policies aimed at harnessing the potential of the sector.

In 1996 the government introduced a comprehensive agricultural policy entitled 'Agriculture Policy 1996 – 2000'. This policy caused more technical and structural problems than solve agricultural problems. This policy was reviewed and a new agriculture policy entitled 'National Agriculture and Livestock Policy 2001 – 2012' was consequently approved in 2002. This policy was framed against the backdrop of the Medium Term Development Strategy 1997 – 2002 and the National Charter on Reconstruction and Development 2000 – 2002. Both these documents contained the government's vision for national and rural development through institutional and physical infrastructure reform.

The main policy areas being addressed by the new Agriculture Policy are:

- Sectoral policies relating to economic and other policies specific to the sector;
- Commodity policies relating to policies focused on expanding production on a sustainable basis;
- Other development policy issues relating to inter-sectoral and interacting policies and compliance; and
- Monitoring and evaluation policies relating to performance requirements of the sector.

Generally, the overall policy thrust is to increase sustainable production and productivity through improved research, extension and development.

In the area of research and development of PGRFA, the Agriculture Policy seeks to promote this activity through collaboration which would lead to accelerated productivity. The government seeks to strengthen the work of special agricultural research institutes such as NARI, the PNG Oil Palm Research Association, Cocoa and Coconut Research Institute and the Coffee Research Institute. All these institutions will be encouraged to develop cutting edge technologies to enhance sustainability in the agriculture sector.

The Agriculture Policy affects biodiversity in two main ways. The first is through the genetic modification of food crops (biotechnology). And second, the introduction of new food crops in the country. The single most important concern for the application of these two methodologies is the biological consequences of these crops when they are released into the environment. Issues of contamination, ethics, IPR and benefit sharing are also crucial in the application of these two approaches. These are issues which will best be dealt with by an ABS framework.

The goals of the Agriculture Policy will be strengthened and enhanced by the new MTDS 2005-2010. The current government has adopted as one of its core development strategy for the period 2005 – 2010 the promotion of agriculture. However, it has decided to abandon the Agriculture Policy and has proceeded through the Department of Agriculture and Livestock to formulate a new National Agriculture Plan that will encapsulate the goals of the MTDS. A draft National Agriculture Plan has been completed and is currently being presented to the public through regional workshops for comments.

Policies on ABS

The issue of ABS has been separated from the general discussion on biodiversity because of its complexity. ABS involves issues of access meaning PIC, benefit sharing and also IPR. The five national policies which were discussed above do not make either explicit or implicit reference to ABS. The policy review shows that there are two draft policies which make special mention about ABS – the draft Sustainable Mining Policy 2003 and the draft Biosafety and Biotechnology Policy 2005. These two documents provide useful principles and guidelines in framing an ABS framework.

Draft Sustainable Mining Policy

The draft Sustainable Mining Policy is quite innovative as it attempts to introduce the concept of sustainability in the mining sector. The greening of the sector will also see the replacement of the Mining Department with a Mineral Resources Authority. Two interesting aspects of the draft mining policy which are relevant for consideration are:

1. Prior informed Consent; and
2. Benefit Sharing

The draft policy promotes the integration of the PIC concept in the mining process at the earliest point of intervention – exploration. Under the draft policy, PIC will become a mandatory aspect of the mining process. Unlike in the past where PIC would be critical prior to development, the draft policy seeks to make it mandatory for PIC to be obtained prior to actual exploration. The draft policy also acknowledges that PIC must be based on "informed consent", thus, it seeks to create a register of independent consultants who can be engaged to provide independent advice to the landowners to enable them to make an informed decision.

Access to the mineral resources will be regulated through the existing legal framework. That is, through the Development Forum and a series of contractual arrangements between the key stakeholders. However, PIC will be the determinant factor for access. In relation to benefit sharing, the draft policy seeks to introduce fundamental conceptual and practical changes to the existing benefit sharing regime.

A crucial component of the new benefit sharing arrangement is that landowners will be identified through social mapping studies and each and every landowner will be paid land compensation directly. This compensation payment to each of the individual landowner can also be paid in kind or part of it can be used to buy shares in the mining venture.

The changes proposed by the draft policy will impact on the *Mining Act*, the *Organic Law on Provincial Governments and Local-level Governments* (OLPGLLG) 1995, the *Provincial Governments Administration Act* 1997, the *Local-level Governments Administration Act* 1997 and the *Environment Act* 2000. The policy and legislative changes will most likely follow the path taken by the Oil and Gas sector.

The draft mining policy is currently under review. It is envisioned that it will be adopted by the government and the Parliament.

Draft Biosafety and Biotechnology Policy

In 2003, the government through the assistance of the United Nations Environment Program (UNEP) and the Global Environment Facility (GEF), PNG began to actively participate in the UNEP/GEF Biosafety Project. The objective of the project was to develop a national biosafety framework for participating countries including PNG. After a series of reviews and consultative workshops over a period of three years, a draft biosafety and biotechnology policy was adopted in 2005.

There are nine objectives of the draft biosafety and biotechnology policy. Four of the objectives are pertinent to ABS. These are:

- ensure the safe handling, use and management of genetically modified organisms for the safety of human health and biodiversity protection in PNG;
- strengthen national institutions engaged in the research and development of genetically modified organisms particularly for food, food processes and pharmaceuticals which contribute to the health and well-being of Papua New Guineans and their environment;
- regulate the trade in genetically modified organisms that may have harmful effects on the health of Papua New Guineans and their environment and biodiversity; and
- facilitate the active participation of local communities in the use, management and transfer of genetically modified organisms that may have an impact on their biological resources and their communities.

The policy seeks to protect resource owners whose biological resources will be accessed for scientific research and for development of genetically modified organisms which have the potential to be commercialized. The policy adopts a series of strategies to achieve this objective. They include:

- public awareness about the benefits and adverse effects of biosafety and biotechnology;
- protection of traditional biological knowledge relating to biosafety and biotechnology through relevant legal mechanisms;
- training of Papua New Guineans in the area of biosafety and biotechnology; and
- provision of tangible assistance to biological resource owners to build their capacity to enable active participation in the ABS process relating to biotechnology.

The draft biosafety and biotechnology policy is expected to be presented to the National Executive Council for endorsement and consequently presentation to Parliament for approval before the end of 2006.

These two draft policies have paved the way for the formulation of a national ABS framework. The lack of an ABS policy has resulted in the government adopting a piecemeal approach towards ABS. The formulation of and adoption of an ABS framework will arrest this piecemeal approach and provide a consistent and strong framework for the access to the country's biological resources and the fair and equitable distribution of benefits arising from the sustainable use of these resources.

Summary

The CBD calls for experts and representatives from the private and public sectors, government officials, representatives from indigenous groups and communities to come together and formulate a policy dealing specifically with ABS. This process is also needed in PNG. The primary concern for policy-makers is to devise a framework to establish, promote and strengthen an ABS framework that encourages the equitable and fair sharing of benefits arising from the sustainable use of biological diversity.

Consideration of issues leading to the framing of a policy is an integral part of modern governments. Before a policy is drafted, problems have to be identified and these must be problems that affect the national interest or more specifically, the lives of the people. Developing policies relating to the environment as well the sustainable use of the resources is very important. For a developing country such as PNG whose resources is in abundance, policies relating to the environment and generally the biodiversity of the country is important. The approach the governments have embarked on since independence has been the incremental approach. This has resulted in governments making changes but not really identifying the core problems and issues relating to a problem. This may be a result of the typical characteristics of governments who lack the capacity to identify and formulate policies that have lasting effects.

The policies which have been reviewed reveal that biodiversity issues are considered in the development programs of PNG. Biodiversity issues are spread out thinly throughout the various sectors. Apart from the draft Mining Policy and Biosafety and Biotechnology Policy, most of the policies, such as the National Goals and Directive Principles; the Environment Policy; the Agriculture Policy; and the Forestry Policy do make explicit mention of certain components of biodiversity and to some extent biodiversity generally.

The draft Mining Policy and Biosafety and Biotechnology Policy do pave the way for the formulation of an ABS regulatory framework. The underpinning of both policies is that traditional resources owners and their biological resources must be respected and that where their resources are required for development, they must be given fair and equitable share of the benefits. The underlying issue would be the level of and the weight the government through its agencies will give to biodiversity conservation and sustainable use albeit ABS in the development planning process. The review shows that biodiversity issues must be seriously integrated into the planning processes. When ABS is integrated in the planning processes with a clear link between the various development goals and ABS, ABS can contribute positively to the attainment of national development goals.

The other option is of course, to develop a specific national biodiversity policy. This national biodiversity policy when developed can cover a wide range of issues ranging from ABS to IPR.

Chapter 6. Accessing Natural Resources and Sharing the Benefits: The Legal Framework

Dr. Eric Kwa and John Kouni

Introduction

The issue of participation, access and sharing of benefits derived from natural resources utilization is synonymous to PNG as well as among other first nation peoples and governments around the world. Article 15 of the CBD reiterates the sovereign rights of States over their natural resources and declares that national governments have the sole authority to permit access to genetic resources. In PNG, ABS is not a new concept, although its application to genetic resources provides a new challenge. Principles of ABS find their origin in the *Constitution*, particularly the second and fourth goals of the NGDP. National practice on ABS has been institutionalised by both legislative enactments and other contractual agreements.

The general principles on which access is permitted, namely mutually agreed terms and prior informed consent form the golden fabric on which the ABS framework and potential guidelines should be based for further development. In PNG, ABS issues vary and can be located in certain pieces of legislation and contractual agreements relating mostly to natural resource exploitation. These laws are either specific or general in nature and scope. What is however lacking is a general ABS regime based on effective and fair legal framework that is encompassing and applicable to all natural resources development.

Designing a fair and workable ABS framework is a huge challenge because ABS issues are sometimes complicated and extremely contentious, cause for disagreement, and even strife. The overwhelming interest by both national and multi-national corporations and investors to explore and exploit the natural resources in PNG urgently demands an effective ABS legal frame work at the national level consistent with international law in order to balance the interest of all stakeholders. An effective ABS legal framework should embrace not only development of natural resources in-situ, public/private sector investments in biodiversity-based innovation and market-based incentives, but also recognise customary ownership and participatory rights of indigenous people.[37] The benefit sharing aspect of ABS needs to be conceptualised in both monetary and non-monetary benefits over a range of temporal scales.

The Legal Framework

The legal framework relating to ABS is closely associated with the subject of participation and natural resources exploitation which is intricately linked to stakeholder partnership. This chapter will focus on the existing legal framework relating to participation and partnership and their relationship to ABS. The laws that will be reviewed include the *Constitution*, the OLPGLLG, the *National Parks Act* 1982, the *Conservation Areas Act* 1978, *Fauna (Protection and Control) Act*, the *International Trade (Fauna and Flora) (Amendment) Act* 2003, the *Environment Act* 2000, the *Forestry Act* 1991, the *Fisheries Management Act* 1998, the *Mining Act* 1992 and the *Oil and Gas Act* 1998.

The Constitution

The *Constitution* and the Organic Laws (Constitutional law) is the supreme law in PNG. All other laws that are inconsistent with the constitutional law are, to the extent of that inconsistency, invalid and ineffective. The Preamble to the *Constitution* outlines the basic framework for access to genetic resources and participation in development. For purposes of this Chapter, only Goal 2 and Goal 4 of the NGDP are pertinent.

Goal 4 of the *Constitution* is in the following terms:

> We declare our fourth goal to be for Papua New Guinea's natural resources and environment to be conserved and used for the collective benefit of us all, and be replenished for the benefit of future generations.
> WE ACCORDINGLY CALL FOR —
> (1) wise use to be made of our natural resources and the environment in and on the land or seabed, in the sea, under the land, and in the air, in the interests of our development and in trust for future generations; and
> (2) the conservation and replenishment, for the benefit of ourselves and posterity, of the environment and its sacred, scenic, and historical qualities; and
> (3) all necessary steps to be taken to give adequate protection to our valued birds, animals, fish, insects, plants and trees.

Goal 4 postulates several key principles of sustainable development which are of relevance to ABS. These include:

- intra-generational equity (poverty alleviation)

[37] Most, if not all, natural resources in PNG are extracted from unalienated land, for further discussion See, Yapao G., "Recognition of Resource Owners Rights and Interests" in Kwa, E (ed)., *Law of Natural Resources of Papua New Guinea* (Sydney: Law Book Co, 2001) 168.

- inter-generational equity (future generations)
- precautionary principle
- fair and equitable sharing of benefits (collective benefit)
- biodiversity conservation

The aim of Goal is therefore sustainable development through the wise use of the country's natural resources. This Goal must be read closely with Goal 2. Goal 2 is in the following terms:

> We declare our second goal to be for all citizens to have an equal opportunity to participate in, and benefit from, the development of our country.

At the core of Goal 2 is equality in participation for development and the fair and equitable sharing of benefits arising from the process of participatory development. The *Constitution* therefore calls for every effort to be made to achieve an equitable distribution of incomes and other benefits of development among individuals and groups throughout the various parts of the country.

Although s25(1) of the *Constitution* declares that the NGDP (including Goal 2) are non-justiciable, Goal 2 is strengthened by s37 (equality before the law) and s55 (equality of all citizens). These two provisions of the *Constitution* provide substantive support for Goal 2. Thus when Goal 2 and 4 are read together, it is clear that every Papua New Guinean must be given an equal opportunity to participate in the development of natural resources located on his or her land and that each person must obtain a fair and equitable share of the benefits accruing from the utilization of these natural resources.

It can be argued that where a person is prohibited or restricted from participating in the development of his or her natural resources and that person is denied benefits derived from the use of his or her natural resources that person can invoke either s37 or 55 of the *Constitution* to exercise his or her rights contained therein. When the law is construed this way, it is suggested that citizen participation in development and fair and equitable sharing of benefits from development are constitutional rights which can be enforceable in a court of law.

OLPGLLG

This Organic Law was introduced in 1995 to sweep away the old provincial government system and establish a reformed system with local-level governments at its core.[38] Under the previous Organic Law, provincial governments did have limited legislative powers to make laws on limited

[38] Regan, A, Jessep, O and Kwa, EL (ed)., *Twenty Years of the Papua New Guinea Constitution* (Sydney: Law Book Co, 2001)

aspects of biodiversity. The new Organic Law has however, removed that power and transposed it on the local-level governments.[39] The absence of a national legal framework on biodiversity use and management has enabled some of the local-level governments to invoke their powers under the OLPGLLG to initiate local-level biodiversity laws.

Local-level governments are mandated under s44 of the Organic Law to enact a wide range of laws on various subject matters. In the area of biodiversity, local-level governments can make laws on: (1) the environment; (2) sacred sites; (3) domestic animals and (4) traditional copyright. Several local-level governments throughout the country have already proceeded to exercise their legislative powers under this provision. On the subject of environment, five local-level governments have already passed laws on the matter. These are the Huhu Local-level Government in Milne Bay Province, the Almami Rural Local-level Government in the Madang Province, the Talasea Local-level Government, the Hoskins Local-level Government and the Bialla Local-level Government.

The Huhu law is very brief and only makes declaratory statements about the environment. There are no substantive provisions on biodiversity use. The Almami, Talasea, Hoskins and Bialla laws are more comprehensive and structured. These laws promote sustainable development by integrating modern and traditional concepts of natural resources use and management. An ABS framework must be flexible so that traditional practices relating to access and management of natural resources which are protected under these local laws are protected and strengthen.

The key provisions on participation and benefit sharing under this law are sections 115, 116 and 98. Section 115 of the Organic Law makes it mandatory for the participation of all the stakeholders in the development of natural resources located within their area. The implementation of this initiative has however been curtailed by s116 which clearly states that an enabling law must clarify the manner of participation. Such a law has not yet been enacted by Parliament.

Section 98 is concerned with benefit sharing from the development of natural resources. An essential term that has been clarified by the Organic Law is 'natural resource'. According to s98(1) the term is defined as:

> Natural resource includes minerals, petroleum, gas, marine products, water, timber (including forest products), fauna, flora and any other product determined by law to be a natural resource.

This definition clearly embraces biodiversity. In this context then, any benefits derived from the development of a biological resource would fall

[39] Environment Act 2000 for example, restricts the power of provincial governments on environmental law-making only to noise pollution.

within the ambit of this provision. The provision specifies the kind of benefits that has to be paid to local-level and provincial governments and explains how resource owners' benefits are to be dealt with under relevant agreements. The model adopted by the Organic Law is based on the arrangements applied in large scale mining and logging projects. Although benefit sharing arrangements between stakeholders in mining, petroleum and logging projects are governed by contract law, s98(2) of the Organic Law makes it mandatory for different levels of benefits to be paid to the different stakeholders. For provincial and local-level governments the following fees are to be paid each fiscal year by a developer of natural resources:

- infrastructural development levies; and
- economic development and land use follow-up levies; and
- community and social development levies; and
- any other levies as are from time to time determined by national law or by agreement.

The following benefits are to be paid by the developer each fiscal year to resource owners:

- royalties;
- landowner premiums;
- compensation; and
- other assistance provided by law or in an agreement.

The Organic Law does not define the term 'royalties' or 'landowner premiums', 'compensation' nor 'other assistance'. The Organic Law also prohibits the direct access to these benefits by resource owners by providing that they will be controlled by the three levels of government through the creation of trust funds. Moreover, these benefits will only be disbursed to the resources owners after deductions have been made for the payment of nominal tax and other 'costs' incurred by the three levels of government.

The main setback for s98(2) is that it requires an Act of Parliament to bring it into force. However, even without the relevant Act of Parliament, developers in the petroleum sector are now required under the *Oil and Gas Act* to implement s98(2) and s115. The principles of sections 98, 115 and 116 of the OLPGLLG are retained by s2 of the *Oil and Gas Act*.

The exposition of the principles in s2 is enlightening given the absence of an enabling legislation required under sections 116 and 98(6) of the Organic Law. The various natural resources development contracts executed between the different parties involved in such projects spell out the benefits that emanate from the development of these resources. These contracts are usually confidential and not open to scrutiny by the public, thus no firm comment can be made about the value and types of benefits that accrue to resource owners. The challenge is to implement section 98(6) and 116 of the

Organic Law through the enactment of a legislation that clearly sets the benchmarks for rates, management, sharing arrangement, and other development benefits.

The National Parks Act

The *National Parks Act* was enacted into legislation in 1982.[40] This legislation gives effect to the World Heritage Convention[41]. The objective of the Act is twofold; firstly to provide for the preservation of the environment and national heritage by: the conservation of sites and areas having a particular biological, topographical, geological, historical, scientific or social importance; and the management of those sites and areas, in accordance with the fourth goal of the National Goal and Directive Principles.[42] It amicably provides for the protection of biodiversity and does allow for sustainable use of biological resources found in national parks.

National parks are controlled and managed by the Director of National Parks who is usually the Secretary for the Department of Environment and Conservation (DEC). The duties of the Director are spelt out in s8 of the Act which include; (1) controlling, managing, and developing any area committed under the Act and (2) encouraging public use and enjoyment of the areas under his or her care. These duties are however restricted only to those areas established under the Act. The Act further permits the Director to erect park use buildings and to develop the national park only for public use and enjoyment. Unlike in other jurisdictions, where development of resources such as mining and forestry can occur in national parks under prescribed circumstances, the *National Parks Act* is silent on these issues. Under s7(1)(a) of the *National Parks Regulation*:

> A person on a reserve, must not dig, cut, collect, remove or interfere with any sand, soil, clay, gravel, rock mineral, shell, fossil, timber (whether or not living), humans or other natural substances or objects whether on or under water, except with the consent of the Director.

It is suggested that in relation to minerals, this provision applies only to the process of investigation by an individual, and such an investigation is probably restricted to personal and educational purposes. The cutting of timber permitted in this provision is also limited to possibly domestic purposes. It is not directed at commercial logging or other similar activities inconsistent with the purpose and intention of the Act. A vital element of

---

[40] It was a Pre-indepedence regulation

[41] Convention for the Protection of the World Cultural and National Heritage

[42] The use of the terms such as biological, topographical, geological, historical scientific and national inheritance by the Act may be traced to the UNESCO *Convention for the Protection of the World Cultural and National Heritage.* Although PNG was not a party to the World Heritage Convention when the treaty was adopted, it has now ratified the treaty and is thus, a party to that treaty.

this provision is that the Director must give his or her consent before an activity can be undertaken. The exercise of his or her discretion is not subjected to any formal guidelines except that his or her discretion must be exercised within the scope of his or her responsibilities as enshrined under s8 of the Act.

The Act does therefore allow for access to national parks but only with the permission of the Director of National Parks. Apart from access for public enjoyment of the national park, access can be given for research in the national park. The law is however silent on the nature and purpose of research. The Act is also is silent on access to genetic resources in national parks for development using biotechnology and the sharing of benefits that may arise from the development of the biological resources. It is imperative to observe that any benefits arising from biological resources obtained from national parks will be exclusive to the State and the developer because national parks are usually situated on State land.

Conservation Areas Act

The *Conservation Areas Act* 1978 is a significant piece of legislation that provides *inter alia* for the preservation of the environment and of the cultural inheritance. This is achieved by the conservation of sites and areas having particular biological, topographical, geological, historic, scientific or social importance; and the management of those sites and areas. The nucleus of the *Conservation Areas Act* is aimed primarily at biological, historical and scenic areas located on customary land unlike the *National Parks Act* which is targeted at State land or customary leased land.

This therefore means that the fundamentally the implementation of the Act rests with the customary landowners. The Act empowers the landowners to make decisions about their land themselves; hence distinguishing it from the *National Parks Act* and *Fauna (Protection and Control) Act.*

Section 4 establishes the National Conservation Council which comprises of not less than five members, who must have technical or special knowledge in relation to matters likely to be put before the Council. Despite the enactment of the legislation in 1978, the Act was not brought into force until 2003 when the Council was established to implement the Act.

The Act provides a meticulous procedure for establishing conservation areas. The process involves:

- request to the Minister for DEC for the establishment of a conservation area;
- investigation of the area to establish biological, topographical, geological, historical, scientific or social significance or other special value for the present community or for future generations by DEC;

- submission to NEC for declaration of conservation area
- declaration of conservation area
- establishment of conservation area management committee
- appointment of conservation rangers

When the conservation area is established its management will be vested in the Conservation Area Management Committee created under s25 of the Act. Any person or an organization who wishes to access biological resources in a conservation area for research and development would have to apply to the Conservation Area Management Committee for approval. When access is approved, the person or organization has to comply with the rules of the Conservation Area and also the Management Plan when conducting research and other activities in the conservation area.

Any development or alteration of the conservation area is restricted to activities consistent with the conservation area's management plan.[43] The Minister is vested with the authority to approve, approve with conditions or deny approval of any proposed development application.[44] Access by the landowners to the natural resources within the declared conservation area would therefore be restricted and subject to the approval by the Minister.

The *Conservation Areas Act* is silent on access to biological resources for development. Access to the conservation area for sightseeing and tourism purposes are covered by the legislation. Access for research and development is not clear under the Act. It is likely that the Conservation Council may introduce rules about ABS relating to biological resources located in conservation areas. However, given that such a mechanism has not yet been developed by the Conservation Council, it is imperative that a national ABS framework which can apply to conservation areas be formulated and adopted by the government.

Fauna (Control and Protection) Act

The *Fauna (Protection and Control) Act* targets the control and management of certain fauna species which are protected under the Act. It originates from the *Fauna (Protection and Control) Regulation* of 1968. This Act is small in scope and yet is very fundamental for biodiversity protection and management. It enables the Minister to declare any fauna species as protected species and also provides for the establishment of protected zones for the protection of certain fauna species.[45] The Act seeks to protect and

---

[43] Section 33 of the Act outlines the duties of the Minister where he has received the application.

[44] See Section 34 of the Act

[45] Historically wildlife areas were set aside for sporting purposes. A person would be permitted by licence to enter the wildlife area and hunt for game. Wildlife law has four main goals. First is to facilitate the sustained periodic harvest of wildlife,

control the harvesting and destruction of fauna. The administration of the Act is vested in the Conservator who is appointed by the Minister under section 4 of the Act.

Section 6 of the Act enables the Minister to declare any fauna as a protected fauna.[46] Any fauna so declared is deemed under s7 as the property of the State. The Act prohibits the killing and possession of a protected fauna. According to s23 the Minister is authorised by the Act to exempt a person or a class of people from this prohibition by a notice in the *National Gazette.* The only qualification is that they are required to kill and catch the fauna using traditional methods. They are not allowed to use firearms to kill the fauna.

The Act also allow for the establishment of sanctuaries established under section 11; protected areas created by s13 and WMAs provided for under s15. Protected areas are declared only for a specific class of protected fauna, while WMA are established for classes of protected fauna. The ten WMA formally established under the legislation are: (1) Bagai WMA; (2) Garu WMA; (3) Maza WMA; (4) Mojirau WMA; (5) Pokili WMA; (6) Ranba WMA; (7) Siwi-Utame WMA; (8) Tonda WMA; (9) Crown Island WMA and (10) Balek WMA. Three sanctuaries (Balek Wildlife Sanctuary, Crown Island Wildlife Sanctuary and Ranba Wildlife Sanctuary) have been declared so far under the Act. These areas are safe haven for endangered or threatened fauna that are declared protected[47] under s6 of the Act. Although the administration of the Act is vested in the Conservator, any effective implementation of the legislation requires meaningful participation of the customary landowners.

Access to protected fauna in sanctuaries, protected areas and WMA require the permission of the Conservator of Fauna who is usually the Secretary for DEC. In the case of WMA the approval is given after consultation with the WMA Committee. Generally, the Secretary is mandated by sections 28 and 29 of the Act, to permit individuals and organizations to take, kill and collect fauna for research.

The other critical issue is whether the Secretary can approve access for research in other biological species? It is suggested that because a sanctuary, protected area and WMA are contained within a specified land area, and the Secretary is empowered by the Act to permit access into these restricted areas, the Secretary can allow for research into other biological species so

second, regulate human behaviour, third, to favour a particular group or groups and fourth, to respect the rights of the animals. These goals are clearly covered by the *Fauna (Protection and Control) Act.*

[46] This mechanism is invoked by the Minister where the fauna is rare or is usually in danger of extinction.

[47] Section 7 of the Act declares that all protected fauna are the property of the State.

long as the research is conducted within the confines of the sanctuary, protected area or WMA. Any research conducted in areas adjacent to a sanctuary, protected area or WMA require access approval from the relevant owners of those areas.

Generally, access to biological diversity varies in context and method depending on the type of biological resource being accessed and assessed. Basically the protected areas law allows for research in biological diversity. PIC is usually obtainable from DEC. These laws however, fall short on dealing with issues of benefit sharing and IPR where a biological resource has the potential to be commercialised.

International Trade (Fauna and Flora) (Amendment) Act

This legislation amended the *International Trade (Fauna and Flora) Act.* It was enacted in 2003 in order to meet the country's obligation under the Convention on the International Trade in Endangered Wild Species of Fauna and Flora (CITES).[48] Basically, the Act controls the export, re-export and import of species protected under Schedules 1, 2, 3,[49] 4, 5 and 6. Exports and imports of these species can only be allowed with a permit issued by the Management Authority which under s3A is the Secretary for DEC.

The Schedules to the Act provide indicators for the dealing in endangered fauna and flora. Schedule 1 contains the latest species list in Appendix I of the Convention. Schedule 2 enumerates the latest species list in Appendix II and Schedule 3 contains the latest species list in Appendix III of the Convention. Three new Schedules have been created under the legislation. These are Schedules 4, 5 and 6. Schedule 4 contains a list of native species that are exempted from the permit requirements; and Schedule 5 contains a list of exotic species that are exempted from permit requirements. Schedule 6 merely adopts the text of the Convention without the Appendices.

The revision of the legislation now means that the Minister can amend Schedules 1 to 5 of the Act without having to seek the approval of the Parliament. The new Act also authorises the Minister under Part 1A to appoint inspectors drawn from other State agencies to assist DEC in the enforcement of the legislation.

The export and import of biological species covered by the Convention identified in PNG would have to comply with the legislation. The legislation also for the first time enables the exportation of native and exotic species

---

[48] According to the CITES Standing Committee if PNG did not enact the amendment, it could have suspended PNG's right to trade in wildlife species because Parties to CITES had revised the list under the Convention.

[49] formerly Appendix I, II, and III respectively

without a permit under the Act. Both Schedules 4 and 5 however, make it explicitly clear that exporters of species listed in these two Schedules are required to obtain approvals under other relevant legislation.

The intention of the Act is not to regulate access and benefit sharing from endangered flora and fauna. The Act explicitly provides that its purpose is to controls the export, re-export and import of species protected under Schedules 1, 2, 3, 4, 5 and 6. Exports and imports of these species can only be allowed with a permit issued by the Secretary for DEC. The export of endangered species of flora and fauna that fall under the ambit of the *International Trade (Fauna and Flora) (Amendment) Act* must comply with the provisions of this legislation.

Does this mean that ABS is not permitted under the Act? On the contrary, the scheme of the legislation allows for the creation of MTA that would regulate ownership, use and management of the endangered biological resources which is the subject of import/export or re-export/re-import. The MTA should spell out clearly the purpose for which the biological material is being exported/imported or re-exported/re-imported, ownership of the material, access to third parties, research and development and benefit sharing.

The nature, content and context of the MTA should be guided by an ABS framework. The formulation of an ABS regime would clarify some of the issues outstanding under the Act.

Environment Act

The *Environment Act* was enacted in 2000 and after four years, it came into force in January 2004. This legislation repeals the *Water Resources Act*, the *Environmental Planning Act* and the *Environmental Contaminants Act*. The objectives of the Act under s4 include: (1) promoting the wise management of PNG's natural resources for the collective benefit of the whole nation and ensure renewable resources are replenished for future generations; (2) protecting the environment while allowing development in a way that improves the quality of life and maintains the ecological processes on which life depends; (3) sustaining the potential of natural and physical resources to meet the reasonably foreseeable future generations, and safeguard the life-supporting capacity of air, water, land and eco-systems; and (4) ensuring that proper weight is given to both long-term and short-term social, economic, environmental and equity considerations in deciding all matters relating to environmental management, protection, restoration and enhancement.

Several strategies have been adopted by the legislation to enable the achievement of these objectives. These include: (1) research on biodiversity; (2) introduction of Environmental Codes of Practice, Environment Protection Orders, Clean-up Orders and Emergency Directions for Level 1 activities; (3) imposition of conditionalities on licences and negotiations on environmental improvement plans and environmental management programs for Level 2 and 3 activities; (4) public participation in projects of national interest; and (5) conduct of environmental impact assessment.

In implementing these strategies, the State and its instrumentalities are vested with the responsibility of ensuring that the following matters of national interest are taken into account:

- preservation of PNG's traditional social structures;
- maintenance of sources of clean water and subsistence food sources to enable Papua New Guineans who depend upon them to maintain their traditional lifestyles;
- the protection of areas of significant biological diversity and the habitats of rare, unique or endangered species;
- the recognition of the role of landowners in decision-making about the development of the resources on their land; and
- responsible and sustainable economic development.[50]

Section 5 expressly makes provision for the protection of biodiversity and endangered biological species. It also recognises the important role and position of landowners in the process of development and obligates the State to involve them in the development of natural resources located on their land.

When dealing with biodiversity conservation and sustainable use under the *Environment Act* 2000, sections 5, 6 and 7 would play a prominent role in this endeavor. Any intervention for biodiversity conservation would have to be at the point where: (1) Environmental Codes of Practice and Environment Protection Orders are developed for Level 1 activities; (2) where licences and negotiations on environmental improvement plans and environmental management programs for Level 2 and 3 activities are being considered or formulated; where public hearing are held for projects which are of national interest; or where an environmental impact assessment is being processed.[51]

---

[50] Section 5 of the Environment Act 2000

[51] Apart from these provisions, there are also three key subordinate legislative enactments approved in 2002 which complement the *Environment Act* to protect the environment. The *Environment (Permits) Regulation* 2002, *Environment (Prescribed Activities) Regulation* 2002 and *Environment (Water Quality Criteria) Regulation* 2002 clarify some of the issues mentioned by the Act. The *Environment (Permits) Regulation* sets out the forms to be issued under the legislation, the *Environment (Prescribed Activities) Regulation* defines activities that fall under Level 2 and Level 3 and the *Environment (Water Quality Criteria) Regulation* prescribes water standards. Two other regulations were also approved at the same time as the other three, namely; the *Environment (Fees and Charges) Regulation* and the *Environment (Council's Procedure) Regulation* 2002. These two regulations

At these critical intervention points, submissions can be made for: (1) the preservation of PNG's traditional, historical and social structures; (2) maintenance of sources of clean water and subsistence food sources to enable Papua New Guineans who depend upon them to maintain their traditional lifestyles; (3) the protection of areas of significant biological diversity and the habitats of rare, unique or endangered species; (4) access to biodiversity; and (5) benefit sharing.

ABS issues are therefore not directly embraced by the Act, but nevertheless, it is allowable at each of the above intervention points. What is critical is that stakeholders are educated on this matter so that when it is raised at any one of these points, adequate considerations can be given to ABS. It is also important to observe that the provisions of the Act will only become operational when an activity which is permissible under Level 2 or 3 has been approved under another piece of legislation. It is from this perspective that it becomes clearer that ABS issues may have been dealt with under that relevant piece of legislation and that the provisions of the *Environment Act* operate as a safety net so that if ABS is not adequately covered in the first legislation, it can be captured here.

Forestry Act

In 991, PNG introduced a comprehensive Forestry policy and a new *Forestry Act* as a response to the Barnet Report and pressure from international organizations. The Act sets up a comprehensive and complex administrative structure, and is declared to be an exhaustive law in the field of national forestry control and development throughout PNG.[52]

Forestry resources in PNG are found largely on customary land which the State has very little control over. Thus, for the State to access these forestry resources it requires the consent of forest resource owners. The *Forestry Act* provides the methodology for the State to access these resources. The relevant provisions of the law are sections 54 to 60. Section 54 declares that forest resources can only be developed in accordance with the National Forest Plan. And section 55 stipulates that forest resources activities can be conducted on: (1) State land; (2) private leasehold land; (3) private freehold land; and (4) customary land.

Given that the majority of forest resources are found on customary land, it is imperative to consider the process involved in obtaining the consent of forest resource owners for the development of their resources. Section 46 of the Act explicitly recognizes the rights of forestry resources owners.

---

provide for the various fees and charges required under the *Environment Act* and also explain the procedure for conducting the meetings of the Environment Council established by s17 of the Act.

[52] See East New Britian Supreme Court Reference Case No.7 of 1992

Access to forestry resources on customary land is permissible through a contract known as the 'Forest Management Agreement' (FMA) provided under s56 of the Act. The FMA enables the owners of the forestry resources to transfer their rights over their forest resources to the State. The FMA is a standard contract the National Forest Authority has devised for use under the legislation. The FMA enables the transaction of rights from the forest resource owners to the State.

The terms of a FMA are provided by section 58 which includes matters such as: (1) location of the forest area; (2) the volume of merchantable timber in the area and (3) amount of money payable to the forest resource owners and the duration of the contract. In consideration for the transfer, the State pays a certain amount of money to the forest resource owners. The payment of this money is based on a very complicated mathematical formula which an ordinary villager is unable to understand.

The giving of consent by forest resource owners as set out in s57 of the Act is basically for access to their forest resources for logging purposes. The monetary benefit that they receive from the government is very minimal. Benefits sharing arrangements for logging activities are left to the resource owners and the logging company. This gap in the law could have easily been closed by s98 of the OLPGLLG, but unfortunately, due to the absence of the enabling Act under this provision, the parties have been left to their own devices.

Fisheries Management Act

The principal legislation governing the use and management of marine fisheries resources is the *Fisheries Management Act* 1998. This legislation repealed the *Fisheries Management Act* of 1994. The legislation gives effect to the National Goals and Directive Principles, particularly to promote the management and sustainable development of fisheries in PNG.

The Act does not apply to the taking of fish for personal consumption, not for sale or trading or for manufacturing purposes; or for sport or pleasure; or by customary fishing; or by artisanal fishing.[53] Section 3(5) explicitly precludes its application in respect of the area to which the *Fisheries (Torres Strait protected Zone) Act* 1984 applies. Like the *Mining Act* and *Oil and Gas Act*, the *Fisheries Management Act* operates on the premise that fisheries resources belong to the State.

Access to fisheries resources remain in the national government's domain. Unlike forestry, mineral and petroleum resources which are located on customary land, the sea falls within the jurisdiction of the State under the *National Seas Act* 1977. Whilst PNG law has recognized the principles that

[53] Section 3(2)

there may be customary rights to reefs and marine resources, there has never been any recognition of absolute ownership to the sea for all purposes. In other words, customary rights under customary marine tenure do not include the acquisition of exclusive possessory title to the sea but may include ownership of reefs etc. for customary purposes.[54] Although the Act recognizes the rights of customary resource owners under s26, they play very little role on issues of access to the nation's fisheries resources.[55]

Access to fisheries resources encapsulated by the legislation is primarily focused on commercial fishing. The relevant provisions of the Act are sections 33 to 36. Section 33 makes provision for access agreements to be executed between the government and other States and regional economic integration organizations or any fishing association or similar body, or a publicly incorporated company, or an individual. These agreements are usually aimed at large-scale fishing activities for commercial purposes. Access for research of marine biodiversity is not envisioned by this provision. When an individual or corporation is allowed access, he or she must enter into a Fisheries Management Agreements with the State. These contracts between PNG and other States are designed to promote cooperation and coordination of fisheries management. These agreements are different to access agreements. Fisheries Management Agreements may relate to fisheries matters required by an access agreement and may involve observer programs, monitoring, control and surveillance.

Advancing the Principles of ABS in the Minerals Sector

Access to mineral resources in the mining sector and the distribution of benefits from mining activities provides useful insights into the operation of ABS principles in PNG. The operationalization of certain ABS principles under the *Mining Act* and the *Oil and Gas Act* will be assessed to draw on essential values in the formulation of an appropriate national ABS framework.

Mining Act

The Mining Act was enacted in 1992 to consolidate and amend legislation to mining and to repeal various statutes relating to land. Although most minerals are found on customary land in PNG, the PIC of landholders is not required to extract those minerals. This is based on the premise that minerals in PNG are the property of the State. Section 5 declares that all minerals

[54] *Vincent Ulelio and Others v Nelulu Land Group and Others* [1998] PNGLR 31

[55] Fisheries Management Act, Section 26 provides that, The rights of the customary owners of fisheries resources and fishing rights shall be fully recognised and respected in all transactions affecting the resource or the area in which the right operates.

existing on, in or below the surface of any land in PNG, including any minerals contained in any water lying on any land in PNG, are the property of the State. The Act further declares under s6 that all land in PNG, including all water lying over that land, is available for exploration and mining and the grant of tenements over it.

In a similar vein the State does not require the PIC of resource owners before it issues a mining tenement over an area of the country. However, although the State owns all the minerals in the country and has the inherent power to issue a mining tenement over any part of the country, it does give *de facto* recognition to landowners' rights over the minerals under s3 of the Act. The recognition of the rights of landowners emanate from their ownership of the land on which a mining tenement is issued. The State does own the minerals but it cannot access these minerals without interfering with the rights of landowners over the use of their land. Section 3 of the Act is in the following terms:

> (1) A development forum shall be convened by the Minister before the grant of any special mining lease to consider the views of those persons whom the Minister believes will be affected by the grant of that special mining lease and shall be conducted by the Minister according to such procedures as will afford a fair hearing to all participants.
>
> (2) The Minister shall invite to a development forum such persons as he considers will fairly represent the views of—
>
> (a) the applicant for the special mining lease; and
>
> (b) the landholders of the land the subject of the application for the special mining lease and other tenements to which the applicant's proposals relate; and
>
> (c) the National Government; and
>
> (d) the Provincial Government, if any, in whose province the land the subject of the application for the special mining lease is situated.
>
> (3) Before the grant of any mining lease the Minister shall consult with the Provincial Government, if any, in whose province the mining lease will be located.

The stakeholders that may be invited by the Minister to a development forum would obviously include landowners. The involvement of the landowners in the mining process only arises where a special mining lease will be granted to a developer of the minerals. A special mining lease is usually issued to the holder of an exploration license who wants to develop a mining project. The perception under the legislation is that landowners have no right to consent to the project and that their involvement is primarily for the purpose of determining what sorts of benefits they will derive from the mining project. These benefits are settled through a string of agreements executed between all the different stakeholders.

The mining development forum is an essential venue whereby stakeholders including the landholders of the subject of the proposed mining lease or tenement have the opportunity for participation in the negotiation affecting the area. The Minister must ensure that the landholders are afforded with a fair hearing.[56] The minister can stop the forum from proceeding if he or she considers that the landholders are not represented by qualified people, or if the resource holders will not be afforded a fair hearing. This recognition by the mining Act in allowing the landholders to participate in the mining development forum a statutory recognition of resource holders' rights and interests to the resources for which the state, by virtue of s6 of the Act claims ownership.[57]

There are two main heads of benefits that can be obtained under the Act: compensation and royalties. Compensation for loss of natural land surface, damage to natural land surface, severance of land, restriction to land, loss or damage to improvements and loss of earnings are covered by Part VII, Division 8 of the Act. Royalties are paid according to the stipulations of s148 of the Act. Participating in the mining project through equity purchase is an important aspect of the mining sector. Other benefits such as infrastructure development, economic development and community and social development are also factored in the mining agreements.

The rules relating to access and the rules governing benefit sharing are very advanced in the mining sector. The draft Sustainable Mining Policy provisions relating to PIC and benefit sharing highlights the seriousness of the sector in improving access and benefit sharing for all the key stakeholders. The new policy acknowledges the special position of landowners and seeks to strengthen their participation in the mining industry by ensuring that they are involved in the initial stages of a mining project – exploration stage. Under the proposed policy, the PIC of landowners must be obtained first to enable access before an exploration is to be initiated in any part of the country.

The ongoing reform in the policy area is however not matched by legislative reform for the mining sector. It highlights the need for a national ABS framework to strengthen the inroads being pursued in the mining sector.

Oil and Gas Act

This legislation was enacted by Parliament in 1998 to replace the *Petroleum Act* amid widespread controversy over issues relating to rights of resource owners. The aim of the legislation is quite comprehensive. It is an Act governing the exploration for and production of petroleum (including oil and

---

[56] Section 3(1).

[57] See Kwa E, Recongnition of Resources owners' rights and interests; in Law of Natural Resources in PNG (ed)___________

gas) in PNG, including the offshore area and, the grant to traditional landowners and Provincial Governments and Local-level Governments of benefits arising from projects for the production of petroleum (including oil and gas), and the processing and transportation in PNG of petroleum and petroleum products. The prominence given to landowners by the legislation reflects the controversy surrounding its enactment.

Like the *Mining Act*, s6 of the *Oil and Gas Act* vests the ownership of all petroleum and helium is vested in the State. Nonetheless, the Act promotes the participation of resource owners at the earliest point of intervention in the industry – exploration. Section 47 imposes a duty on the holder of a petroleum prospecting license to undertake social mapping studies and landowner identification studies during the course of exploration. The scope and method of a social mapping study or landowner identification study shall be prescribed by the Minister for Petroleum and Energy. If a discovery is notified by a licensee and the licensee conducts a final feasibility study of the development or extension of a petroleum project for the production of petroleum from that discovery, the licensee shall at the same time conduct:

> A full-scale social mapping study; and
> A full-scale landowner identification study of customary owners and the occupants of the land which will be comprised in the license area of a petroleum development license or licences which would pertain to the development of that discovery and the land within five kilometers of any facility which would be a dedicated project facility (other than a facility which would be situated on such a petroleum development license) of the petroleum project or other areas which would be affected by the petroleum project if developed.

Once the resource owners are clearly identified, s48 states that they can then be able to participate in a petroleum development forum. The Act makes it mandatory for the Minister to convene a development forum which should be attended by all persons or organisations which the Minister believes will be affected by that petroleum project.[58] All stakeholders in the proposed project are required to meet at this forum to negotiate the terms and conditions of the development project.

Development forums under s48 shall not be convened in respect of a proposed petroleum project until certain conditions are satisfied. One of the crucial conditions is the preparation of the proposal by the Director. A development forum shall not be convened in respect of a proposed petroleum project until the Director has prepared a proposal; after giving due consideration to the results of the full-scale social mapping and landowner identification studies and the socio-economic impact study and the principle set out in s170(3), for the equitable sharing of the equity benefit and the

[58] See section 48(1)(a to f)

royalty benefit amongst project area landowners; and has provided that proposal to representatives of those future project area landowners.

Equally significant is s50 of the Act. This section provides that an agreement between the State and any of the project area landowners, the affected local-level governments and the affected provincial government of a petroleum project must contain all the relevant conditions required by the Act. In addition a development agreement may contain any other matters agreed between the parties.[59] These conditions and the forum required under these provisions allow the landholders of the project area to participate meaningfully in the negotiations process that would eventually determine the benefits they would eventually access to and enjoy from the development.

One of the most tangible benefits that will be realized by the resource owners, provincial and local-level governments and the State are royalty payments. Section 159 states that a tenement holder shall pay to the State royalty at a rate of 2.00% of the wellhead value of all petroleum produced from the license area. The royalty benefit granted is paid monthly[60] and is shared between the project area landowners, the affected local-level governments and the affected provincial governments of the project in proportions agreed by them in an agreement.[61] Section 165 provides for State equity entitlement. Out of the State equity entitlement referred to in s165, a certain portion of the equity benefit is reserved for project area landholders. The equity benefit granted under this section shall be shared between the project area landowners and affected local-level governments of the project in proportions agreed by them in an agreement.

Apart from royalty and equity participation benefits, the State may also provide to or for the benefit of project area landowners or the people of the project area or the people of the region, by way of grants out of consolidated revenue or otherwise, such other benefits in addition to those specified in the Act as the State sees fit.[62] This is an additional provision that may be invoked to maximize the benefit of the landholders of a project area.

Recent Proposals

There are two recent government proposals that are afoot which require mention. The first is the draft Biosafety and Biotechnology Bill 2005 and the second is the draft Maritime Boundaries proposal. Both of these proposals are likely to be implemented within the next 18 months and will have a huge bearing on ABS and therefore need mention.

---

[59] Section 50(2)
[60] Section 168(3)
[61] Section 168(2)
[62] Section 171(1)

Draft Biosafety and Biotechnology Bill

This Bill was promulgated under the UNEP/GEF Biosafety Project which was discussed in Chapter 4. The Bill was drafted in 2004 and after several drafts was final adopted by the stakeholders in 2005. When the Bill was being formulated in 2004, similar pieces of legislation from other parts of the world were reviewed, but no clear examples on the subject were identified. Thus, Part 6 (sections 57-60) of the Bill which relates to ABS was framed to cater for the situation in PNG. Part 6 is the first attempt at operationalizing the Access Benefit Sharing concept in PNG.

Several examples in PNG were considered. These included: (1) the OLPGLLG; (2) the *Mining Act*; (3) the *Oil and Gas Act*; and (4) the draft Sustainable Mining Policy. As highlighted above, these regulatory frameworks do not explicitly provide for an ABS regime. The Bill therefore seeks to set a new paradigm for ABS in PNG. The relevant sections of Bill are set out as follows:

> PART 6. – ACCESS TO GENETIC RESOURCES FOR RESEARCH AND DEVELOPMENT.
>
> 57. ACCESS TO GENETIC RESOURCES.
>
> (1) A person who intends to conduct scientific research for the discovery of genetic materials for the development of genetically modified products shall obtain a licence for such purpose from the Council.
>
> (2) The application for a biodiscovery licence shall be in accordance with Section 31 of this Act.
>
> (3) Where the research activity will be conducted on customary land the applicant shall set out in full the manner in which traditional knowledge of the local communities will be applied and the rights of the holders of traditional knowledge will be protected if the research leads to the development of genetically modified organisms or products.
>
> (4) Where the applicant for research and development is a foreign individual or organization, the applicant shall provide clear and strong guarantees for technology transfer and capacity building in that-
>
> (*a*) it will work together with relevant tertiary or research institutions in Papua New Guinea on the proposed research and development project; and
>
> (*b*) it will fund, train and engage Papua New Guinean scientists in the research and development of the genetically modified organisms and products.
>
> (5) In addition to the matters contained in Section 39 and this section, the Council shall give paramount consideration to the protection and conservation of the cultural values and traditional knowledge and biological diversity of the local communities.
>
> (6) Subject to Section 21, the Council shall fix access fees-
>
> (*a*) to be paid by an applicant under this Part; and

(*b*) remitted to the local community to be shared equally by the local-level government and local communities.

58. PRIOR INFORMED CONSENT.

(1) Where local communities will be directly affected by the biodiscovery project, the prior informed consent of the local communities must be obtained by the applicant and Council before a licence is granted under this Act.

(2) The provincial and local-level governments shall be fully informed of the negotiations between the applicant, the Council and the local communities.

(3) Subject to Subsection (5), the Council may formulate Guidelines specifying the manner in which consent of local communities would be obtained for the purposes of this Act.

(4) The process by which the prior informed consent of the local communities is obtained must be simple, transparent and allow the greatest opportunity for participation by the local communities particularly women and the youths.

(5) The absence of appropriate Guidelines under Subsection (3), does not absolve the Council and the applicant of their duty to seek and obtain the prior informed consent of the local communities before the issuance of a licence under this Act.

59. REGISTER OF CONSULTANTS.

(1) In order to assist local communities participate meaningfully in the negotiations, the Council shall keep a register of consultants who may be called upon to provide social, financial, legal or environmental advice to local communities.

(2) The costs of the consultants shall be covered by the applicant and Council.

(3) The appointment and the terms of references of consultants shall be by mutual agreement between the Council, the applicant and the local communities.

60. BENEFIT SHARING.

(1) The Council shall, before issuing a licence for an activity relating to this Part, ensure that a valid benefit sharing arrangement in the form of a contract is executed between the local communities, the relevant local-level governments, provincial government, the applicant and the Council.

(2) The following principles shall be taken into account by the Council when negotiating benefit sharing agreements-

(*a*) the percentage of royalties negotiated as payments might vary depending on the relationship of the marketed genetically modified product to the original isolated product; and

(*b*) it is understood that the eventual development of a product to the marketing stage is a long term process which may require 10 to15 or more years; and

(*c*) benefit sharing must be on an equitable basis, whether the genetically modified product is based on synthetic or semi-synthetic variations of compounds or structurally based natural products; and (*d*) all scientists and individuals who contribute to the identification and discovery of new genetically modified products such as chemotherapeutics, pharmaceuticals, industrial products or molecular probes or genetic constructs should be compensated in terms of royalties arising from patent agreements; and

(*e*) compensation will include milestone payments at key stages of clinical development; and

(*f*) if a natural product, isolated from a Papua New Guinea source material is developed as a commercial agent, and is required for semi-synthesis of such, then Papua New Guinea should be the first source of the raw material, unless the quality and quantity of material is insufficient for such use; and

(*g*) if prior indigenous knowledge is involved in the collection of samples or development of genetically modified organisms or products, then suitable recognition should be given to this intellectual property in terms of appropriate compensation and patent inventorship status; and

(*h*) should any genetically modified organism eventually be licensed to a commercial enterprise for further development or production and marketing, the interests of Papua New Guinea and the local communities must be adequately taken into account.

(3) In determining the distribution of benefits, the following criteria shall be used as a guide-

(*a*) fifteen percent of the benefits shall be allocated to the local communities; and

(*b*) five percent of the benefits shall be allocated to the local-level government; and

(*c*) three percent of the benefits shall be allocated to the provincial government; and

(*d*) ten percent of the benefit shall be allocated to the State; and

(e) sixty seven percent of the benefits shall be allocated to the applicant.

(4) To ensure that benefits to local communities are equitable and sustainable, the following method of disbursement shall be used as a guide to manage the benefits provided to local communities under Subsection (3)(a)-

(*a*) thirty percent of the benefits will be set aside for future generations to be held in trust and managed by the State; and

(*b*) thirty percent of the benefits shall be allocated for sustainable development projects for the community; and

(*c*) twenty percent of the benefits shall be used for investments; and

(*d*) twenty percent of the benefits may be distributed in cash equitably amongst the members of the local communities.

(5) The benefit sharing agreement shall be executed by the parties whether or not the biodiscovery and the use of biotechnology will

result in the development of genetically modified organisms or in the manufacture of genetically modified products.

(6) Where there are disputes as to ownership of land or other related disputes, the disputing parties must in principle give their consent for the biodiscovery activity to proceed, and in the event that the dispute is procrastinated, the State shall manage the benefits of the local communities until such time as those disputes have been resolved.

Apart from the issue of PIC and the principles which are to be considered in developing an equitable benefit sharing arrangement, Section 60 proposes a bold apportionment of benefits. It takes another step up from the standard set by sections 98 and 99 of the OLPGLLG. The Organic Law provides a framework for the distribution of benefits. Section 60 elevates the process to another level by suggesting concrete figures for the apportionment of benefits.

Another important feature of Part 6 is that the legislation will establish a program whereby local consultants can be registered and called upon to assist the local communities in negotiating deals with potential licence applicants, the Council (and where appropriate, the provincial and local-level governments). These consultants will be paid for by the government and the potential licence applicant. A fee for this purpose may be imposed by the Biosafety and Biotechnology Council. The concept is not new as consultants are already being registered under the *Forestry Act* and the proposal for the government to pay for the consultants is already embedded in the draft Sustainable Mining Policy.

Sections 57 and 60 give recognition to and protect intellectual property rights of traditional owners of biological knowledge. These provisions of the proposed law will protect holders of traditional biological knowledge and also provide a mechanism whereby any financial benefits arising from the use of that knowledge will be distributed to them.

Maritime Zones Project

In December 2004 the Commonwealth Secretariat and the government started working on a discussion paper on maritime zones legislation. The aim of the project is to repeal the *National Seas Act* and the subsidiary legislation, the *Offshore Seas Proclamation* 1978 and also clarify and demarcate the following maritime zones:

- Internal Waters
- Territorial Sea
- Contiguous Zone
- Exclusive Economic Zone (EEZ)
- Continental Shelf
- Extended Continental Shelf

Both parties agreed that the new law should bring PNG into conformity with the UNCLOS and the formulation of the new law should also be consistent with the *Fisheries Management Act* and the *Environment Act*. A key component of the proposal is the creation of marine protected areas. The proposed Bill will make provision for the creation of marine protected areas to implement Article 194(1) of UNCLOS.

The aim of the marine protected area is for the preservation and protection of the marine environment. According to the draft proposal, the creation of marine protected areas is an extension to protected areas created under the *Fauna (Control and Protection) Act*. Marine protected areas may be designated as:

- Fishing Reserves;
- Marine Parks; or
- Marine reserves.

According to the proposal in these areas, the new Act should provide for measures to be taken for the conservation and management of a marine protected area, including: (1) the prohibition of certain activities; and (2) the carrying out of certain activities subject to certain conditions.

The power to permit access and PIC to enter these maritime zones will be vested in the Marine Scientific Research Committee. The new Act will formalize the establishment of the Marine Scientific Research Committee and also broaden and strengthen its work. The Guidelines for Marine Scientific Research Programs in PNG Territorial Waters approved by the National Executive Council in 2003 will also be strengthened under the new proposal.

These proposals will have far reaching effects on the jurisdictions of the DEC, the National Fisheries Authority, provincial and local-level governments and the Mineral Resources Authority and the Department of Petroleum and Energy. Given that the proposal is currently being reviewed, interventions relating to ABS at this stage are imperative.

Conclusion

The ABS concept is not new to PNG, although its application to genetic resources is a new challenge that would require further work. The review of the legal framework reveals that national practice relating to ABS is fairly institutionalized although pragmatic. It is suggested that the constitutional basis of the principles underlying ABS are Goals 2 and 4 of the *Constitution* and sections 98, 115 and 116 of the OLPGLLG.

The various pieces of legislation that have been reviewed have not clearly articulated the underlying principles of Goal 2 and 4 of the *Constitution* relating to access and benefit sharing. Those that have attempted to make that link have fallen short of the objectives of the Constitutional Goals.

Successive governments have however recognised the significance of consultation and partnership particularly with customary resources owners in development project because of the significant impacts of the projects on the livelihoods of the local people and their customary land. Participation by stakeholders in major development projects and particularly in the minerals sector is achieved through developmental forums and other forums that are held after the initial forum. Agreements on access to and the sharing of benefit are usually marked out at these meetings and incorporated in a series of mining agreements. The provisions under the *Mining Act* and *Oil and Gas Act* reflect the importance of participation, mutual agreements and fair and equitable sharing of benefits from mining and petroleum activities. The *Oil and Gas Act* has elevated the PIC issue to another level by giving due recognition to the rights of resource owners in participatory development.

The first real attempt to tackle ABS is manifest in the draft Biosafety and Biotechnology Bill. The scope of the ABS under this new regime is however limited to research and development of genetic resources. The new maritime zones Bill also provides new opportunities for the promotion of ABS.

However, despite these positive developments, there is need for an effective and fair legal framework that goes beyond the existing pieces of legislation to cater for the wider issues of biodiversity. Such a law must promote economic efficiency, while at the same time ensuring fairness, transparency and due process, consideration of the public interest and the rights of various stakeholders, as well as addressing broader social equity and rights issues. Based on such premise, any benefit sharing aspect must be designed and modeled over a range of temporal scale, to cater for financial benefits as well as non monetary benefits. The concept and practice of benefit sharing must not only reflect a balance between the State and developers, but also between landowners and other stakeholders. Only then can a meaningful development be achieved in the country.

Chapter 7. Research and Development of Biodiversity and ABS

Professor Simon Saulei

Introduction

It is generally acknowledged that the potential of large areas of tropical forests, coral reefs, oceans, soils and other remote or largely scientifically unexplored areas remain virtually untapped. Hidden within these tropical ecosystems are many undiscovered organisms that may have properties that can cure diseases, provide new food sources, means to clean polluted environments and better ways to manufacture products used daily in modern society.

This is primarily the issue addressed by access and benefit-sharing in the CBD: the exploration and use of those biological resources could and should serve as an incentive to conserve them and their habitats, as well as providing monetary and technological resources and expertise to do so. Access to genetic resources and benefit-sharing has been one of the most important active themes of the CBD and of which researchers, collaborators and researching institutions must give due recognition to the CBD requirements, especially Article 15. The intention of this so-called "grand-bargain" envisaged in the CBD is to allow biodiverse countries, especially in developing countries like PNG to reap the benefits of their biological resources with contributions to the cost of conservation.

Natural products provide unique and extremely broad biochemical diversity, distinct from those that are found in synthetic or combinatorial chemical libraries currently available and they show an extreme range of activity.

PNG which represents less than 1% of the global land mass is very rich in biodiversity estimated to be between 6-7% of the world's biological diversity. Much of these biodiversity has yet to be scientifically discovered through research and development. However, as explained above, the primary issue yet to be addressed is that of accessing and sharing the benefits arising from research and development of this rich biological diversity. Further, the issues of accessing and sharing of benefits derived of the development of these biological resources, as well as ownership are very critical, since these resources are owned by traditional customary owners and not the state as is the case in other countries.

In order to have access to these biological resources and share the benefits arising from their developments, national research institutions, individuals and their international collaborators should adhere to a number of basic principles set out below because:

- activities involving access to genetic resources and associated traditional knowledge should be consistent with the provisions of the CBD, the CITES and other international, regional and national laws and policies concerning biodiversity;
- states have sovereign rights over their own biological resources and the authority to determine access to genetic resources rests with national governments;
- it is essential to establish conditions that facilitate access and support scientific research, while honouring the principles of prior informed consent and benefit-sharing;
- it is important to share the benefits arising from the use (development) of genetic resources and their derivatives fairly and equitably with the country of origin that provided the genetic resources and other stakeholders, as appropriate;
- it is also critical to honour the terms and conditions under which genetic resources have been acquired; and that
- cooperation among research institutions and governments will facilitate access to genetic resources and benefit sharing.

The purpose of this Chapter is to set out the principles for access and sharing of benefits, mostly focusing on research and development of biological resources to promote a harmonized system amongst the researchers, their institutions, collaborators, governments and the resource owners. The following discussions are adopted from the Common Policy Guidelines for assisting in the preparation of institutional policies based on the Principles of access to genetic resources and benefit sharing (Cartagena, 2000).

Principles for Access to Genetic Resources and Benefit Sharing

Researchers, their institutions and collaborators should adhere to the following principles when accessing genetic resources and sharing benefits when conducting research and development (R&D) of biodiversity in the country.

1. *Convention on CBD and laws related to Access to genetic resources and associated Traditional Knowledge and Benefit-Sharing*

- Comply with the requirements of the CBD, CITES and other international, regional and national laws relating to access and benefit-sharing, including those relating to traditional knowledge.

2. *Acquisition of Genetic Resources*
   - In order to obtain prior informed consent, provide a full explanation of how the genetic resources will be acquired and used.
   - When acquiring genetic resources from *in situ* conditions, obtain prior informed consent from the government of the country of origin and any other relevant stakeholders, according to applicable laws and best practice.
   - When acquiring genetic resources from *ex situ* collections (such as botanical gardens), obtain prior informed consent from the body governing the *ex situ* collection and any additional consents required by such a body.
   - When acquiring genetic resources from ex situ sources, whether from *ex situ* collections, commercial sources or individuals, evaluate available documentation and where necessary, take appropriate steps to ensure that the genetic resources were acquired in accordance with applicable laws and best practice.
3. *Use and Supply of Genetic Resources*
   - Use and supply genetic resources and their derivatives on terms and conditions consistent with those under which they were acquired.
   - Prepare a transparent policy on the commercialization (including plant sales) of genetic resources acquired before and since the CBD entered into force and their derivatives, whether by the participating researcher or institution or a recipient third party.
4. *Use of Written Agreements*
   - Acquire genetic resources and supply genetic resources and derivatives using written agreements, where required by applicable laws and best practice, setting out the terms and conditions under which the genetic resources may be acquired, used and supplied and resulting benefits shared.
5. *Benefit-Sharing*
   - Share fairly and equitably with the country of origin and other stakeholders the benefits arising from the use of genetic resources and their derivatives including non-monetary and in the case of commercialization also monetary benefits.

- Share benefits arising from the use of genetic resources acquired prior to the entry into force of the CBD, as far as possible, in the same manner as for those acquired after the CBD came into force.

6. *Curation*

   In order to comply with these Principles, maintain records and mechanisms to:

   - record the terms and conditions under which genetic resources are acquired;
   - track the use in the participating institution and benefits arising from that use; and,
   - record supply to third parties, including the terms and conditions of supply.

7. *Prepare a Policy*

   - Prepare, adopt and communicate an institutional policy setting out how the participating stakeholders will implement these Principles

These general principles of ABS relating to R&D must drive the formulation of the ABS framework. The challenge is to codify these principles in clear legal terms so that relevant stakeholders benefit fairly in the development of biological resources.

Elaborations on major Principles

Six of the seven principles are discussed in some detail to provide a guide in the formulation of the ABS framework.

Acquisition

There are two important points to note about acquisition. First, the Prior Inform Consent (PIC) of the resource owner or regulator must be obtained by the researcher, their institution and collaborators. Second, the terms and conditions of access must be clarified in a Material Transfer Agreement (MTA). These two factors will provide the roadmap for the future dealings of the stakeholders and the biological resource.

Prior Informed Consent (PIC)

When collecting or gaining access to genetic resources, researches should abide by appropriate international and national laws, regulations and best practice. When obtaining access to genetic resources from *in situ* conditions, researchers, their institutions and collaborators should:

- where needed, in accordance with applicable laws, obtain, in writing, the PIC of the resource owners and government of the country of origin; and must make reasonable and sincere effort to:

- obtain and record the PIC of other stakeholders, as appropriate, for access to and use of the genetic resources concerned and associated knowledge;
- ensure that any collection, import, export and other handling of the genetic resources has been in accordance with all applicable laws; and
- clarify, in writing based on a full explanation of how the genetic resources will be acquired and used, the terms and conditions under which the materials are acquired and can subsequently be used, especially whether the materials or their derivatives may be supplied to third parties or commercialized.

When obtaining access to genetic resources from documented *ex situ* collections, researchers, their institutions and collaborators must:

- obtain, in writing, PIC from an officer authorized to agree with the terms and conditions of access on behalf of the *ex situ* collection, and such other consents required as indicated by that officer for access to genetic resources concerned and for their use; and will make reasonable and sincere efforts to:
- obtain from the authorized officer of the supplier or owner a written statement that the genetic resources were acquired and are being supplied in accordance with all applicable laws and that the supplier or owner is entitled to supply them to the researcher;
- ensure that the export of the genetic resources or their derivatives from the country where the supplier or owner is based, and import to the country where the researcher is based, are in accordance will all applicable laws; and,
- clarify, in writing, based on a full explanation of how the genetic resources will be acquired and used, the terms and conditions under which the materials are acquired and can be subsequently be used, especially whether the materials or their derivatives may be supplied to third parties or commercialized.

When obtaining access to genetic resources from *ex situ* sources other than those stipulated above, for example from commercial sources, owners or individuals, each party should ensure that the acquisition conforms with applicable laws and best practice, and in cases where there is no applicable law, must, where appropriate, evaluate available documentation and make reasonable and sincere efforts to ascertain from the supplier or owner that the materials were obtained in accordance with provisions of the CBD and best practice.

Use of Written Agreements to Clarify Terms and Conditions of Acquisition

When obtaining access to genetic resources, each party will make reasonable and sincere efforts to clarify in writing the respective roles, rights and responsibilities of the researcher, supplier or owner, the country of origin and relevant parties, as appropriate, in activities involving the use of genetic resources.

Use

Researchers, their institutions and collaborators should only use genetic resources for purposes consistent with the terms and conditions under which they are acquired. If a researcher wishes to use such genetic resources for purposes other than those allowed by the terms and conditions under which the material was originally acquired (such as for commercial use when access was granted for non-commercial purposes), the researcher shall obtain approval from the supplier or owner for such use and should specify in writing the terms and conditions of use, including fair and equitable benefit-sharing.

A researcher, his or her institution or collaborators may wish to commercialise genetic resources (or their derivatives) for which the terms and conditions under which they were acquired are not clear. In such a case:

- if the genetic resources were acquired after the entry into force of the CBD, each researcher shall obtain the informed consent of the supplier or owner (or, if the supplier or owner is not known), the country of origin), prior to commercializing the genetic resources, and should specify in writing the terms and conditions of use, including fair and equitable benefit-sharing.
- if the genetic resources were acquired prior to the entry into force of the CBD, each researcher shall share benefits arising from their commercialization according to the benefit-sharing arrangements discussed below, and should clarify, in the policy on commercialization referred to in the Principles, whether, prior to commercialization, they will obtain the informed consent of the supplier or owner (or, if the supplier or owner is unknown, the country of origin).

Curation

Each researcher, institution or collaborator acquiring genetic resources will make reasonable and sincere efforts to record and maintain data on their acquisition, including information on the supplier or owner; country of origin; collector; and if available, dates, accession numbers, taxon names, etc; PIC and terms and conditions of use; and other relevant data associated with acquisition of accessions in its collections.

Each researcher, institution or collaborator will make reasonable and sincere efforts to record and maintain information concerning the use of genetic resources and their derivatives by that researcher and the benefits to that participating researcher, institution arising from such use.

The participating researcher, collaborator and institution will make reasonable and sincere efforts to record and maintain data on the supply of genetic resources and their derivatives, including information on the recipient and the terms and conditions of access and benefit sharing under which they were supplied. When providing genetic resources and their derivatives to a recipient, each participating institution will also provide relevant data on their acquisition to the recipient as described above, particularly information on prior informed consent and conditions of use.

In order to be able to fulfill its commitments, each participating researcher, collaborator or institution will develop and implement appropriate mechanisms to track the acquisition of genetic resources, the different uses of genetic resources and their derivatives held in its collections, their supply to recipients and the benefits that arise from their use.

Each participating institution shall establish systems of staff management and individual responsibilities for the implementation of compliance with the principles.

Supply

Each participating researcher, collaborator or institution may supply, whether by way of a gift, sale or loan, genetic resources or their derivatives to other participating institutions and their third parties for conservation, research and development, public display, education and other purposes.

At the time of supplying genetic resources or their derivatives, each participating researcher, collaborator or institution will, consistent with its policy on commercialization, clarify with the recipient, whether the supply is for commercial or for non-commercial purposes.

When supplying genetic resources or their derivatives, each participating institution, researcher or collaborator will honour any terms and conditions to which it committed when acquiring the genetic resources, such as any terms and conditions set out in written agreements.

To the extent possible, when supplying genetic resources or their derivatives, each participating researcher, collaborator or institution will treat genetic resources acquired prior to the entry into force of the CBD and those acquired after its entry into force in the same manner.

When supplying genetic resources or their derivatives, each participating researcher, collaborator or institution recognizes the need to supply genetic resources under written agreements which obliges each recipient:

- to share benefits arising from its use of the genetic resources and their derivatives fairly and equitably;
- not to commercialise the genetic resources or their derivatives without the explicit consent of the participating researcher, collaborator or institution providing them; and,
- not to pass the genetic resources or their derivatives without ensuring that the third parties enter into written agreements containing terms and conditions that are no less restrictive.

Benefit Sharing

Each participating researcher, collaborator or institution will make reasonable and sincere efforts to share the benefits arising from the use of genetic resources and their derivatives fairly and equitably with the government of the country of origin, the resource owners and other stakeholders as appropriate.

To the extent possible, each participating researcher, collaborator or institution will share the benefits arising from the use of materials acquired prior to and after the entry into force of the CBD in the same manner.

The objective of sharing benefits is to achieve fairness and equity and to create incentives and provide resources for the conservation of biological diversity and the sustainable use of its components.

Benefits which participating institutions, researchers, resource owners and governments will share depending upon what is fair and equitable in the circumstances, including commitments made in written agreements and may include:

- taxonomic, biochemical, ecological, horticultural and other information and data, through research and development results, publications and educational materials;
- access to collections and databases;
- benefits in kind, such as augmentation of national collections in the country of origin and support of community development activities;
- the transfer of technology such as hardware, software and know-how;
- training in science, *in situ* and *ex situ* conservation and management, information technology and management and administration of access and benefit-sharing;
- institutional development, strengthening and management;
- joint research and development, through collaboration in training and research programmes, participation in product development, joint ventures and co-authorship of publications; and,

- in the case of commercialization, also monetary benefits such as royalties.

Other forms of benefits which could be shared amongst the stakeholders are those relating to Patents and Intellectual Property Rights (IPR), which for PNG must be clearly defined in terms of scope and limits on what can be claimed under IPR in accordance with the basic principle of "no ownership of life forms" and the CBD's objectives.

Where IPRs are legitimate and ethical, then the share can be distributed in terms of proportionate royalties or graduated monetary payments at different stages of exchange, research and development of biological diversity. However, beyond IPR, many types of benefits as mentioned above can be creatively developed, including joint venture activities and incentives for research and development.

Current Status of ABS and R&D in Papua New Guinea

The current situation regarding access and benefit sharing by research institutions and their collaborators in the country is such that there are no policies to regulate how genetic resources are used in R&D and commercialization. The University of Papua New Guinea has a brief policy on benefit sharing which recognizes the importance of sharing the benefits with its collaborators, resource owners, national government, students, staff and the institution itself. However, the issue of access has yet to be worked out, apart from the ad hoc arrangements currently in use. These arrangements include the facilitation of individual researchers or international collaborators either through the National Research Institute or the DEC. Most of these arrangements involve obtaining visas, approvals from provincial research committees and exportation of biological materials through DEC (for animals and species under CITES), the PNG Forest Research Institute (for plants) and NAQIA for phytosanitory requirements. In most instances, the approval from the PRC is taken as the prior informed consent for accessing biological resources within the province, but this is a flaw as the resources are neither owned by the provincial nor the National Government, but by the traditional customary owners. Hence, such PIC should be sought from traditional owners and not from the provincial research committees.

Under the Papua New Guinea Institute of Biodiversity (PINBio) and the DEC arrangements, a Material Transfer Agreement (MTA) is required prior to such materials being exported overseas, but this does not involve materials (plants, animals, microbes, etc) being exported outside of such arrangements by other government agencies, NGOs, researchers, individuals or corporate bodies. Thus, what this means is that much of what had and still being exported without the PINBio/DEC MTA arrangements are not being censored in compliance with the CBD, CITES, etc – this is biopiracy.

As a consequence, PNG is loosing a lot of benefits from the development of such materials and their derivates.

Summary

There is an urgent need for the government to establish a national ABS policy and legislation to protect its unique and rich biological diversity as required under the CBD. Such a policy and legislation should incorporate the major Principles mentioned above and should, in no uncertain terms, define where the responsibility of issuing prior informed consent lies, the coordination or approvals of research applications and the arrangements for access to biological materials and equitable benefit sharing. Currently, these ad hoc arrangements have not provided meaningful monetary benefits as well as the associated capacity building and transfer of technology to the resource owners and the country at large. However, if such benefits are actually provided, especially to the resource owners, these would act as incentives for them to appreciate the values of the country's biological resources and in turn provide them the motivations to protect and conserve our natural capital – the rich and unique biological diversity, both for the present and future generations.

Chapter 8. ABS and Intellectual Property Rights

Mange Matui

Introduction

The discussion in this Chapter will focus on IPR and its relationship to ABS. In the other Chapters, issues of access to biological resources, laws and policies relating to access and benefit sharing and relevant principles relating to ABS. IPR issues usually relate to the potential commercialization of the valuable aspects of biological resources. It is therefore essential that issues of IPR is dealt with at the access stage so that the parties are able to agree on the sharing of benefits that arise as a result of the commercialization of the biological resource. The relevant parties and their ownership and rights that may be created by the registration of an IPR must also be agreed upon at the point of access. The potential benefits that may arise because of the registration and commercialization of biological resources and the taxation implications are covered in Chapter 9.

The aim of this Chapter is to provide the legal framework governing IPR in PNG. The crucial issue that will be addressed in this Chapter is the protection of traditional biological knowledge under the present legal regime. Article 15 and 8(j) provide clearly the need for the protection of traditional knowledge relating to biological diversity and the holders of that body of knowledge. Does the present legal regime adequately embrace the principles set out in the two provisions of the CBD? The quick answer to this question is of course negative. Nonetheless, it is imperative to set out the legal framework so that where there are gaps in the law, appropriate measures can be recommended to rectify such gaps.

Intellectual Property Rights: What is it?

It is imperative at this stage to clearly understand the meaning of IPR. IPR are rights given to persons who have used their intellect to discover or develop or create something which usually has economic value (intellectual property). Many countries around the world including PNG have through legislation created property rights for certain products of intellectual effort and ingenuity. Thus, through intellectual property law, the State allows the creator to financially benefit from his creation. This benefit is usually for a certain period of time.

IPR can be divided into two categories namely; copyright and industrial property right. The industrial property right covers the protection of trademarks and other distinctive signs that may be used for commercial purposes. By giving this legal protection to industrial property, it is envisioned that this will stimulate innovation, design and creation of technology. Basically, the conferring of intellectual property is a method of privatizing ownership.

By protecting the owners of intellectual property, the law rewards the owners for their creativity. As to how much the owner stands to gain because of this legal protection depends on the commercial value of the intellectual property.

IPR Related Issues

PNG, like other countries has established a comprehensive legal framework for the registration and protection of IPR. Does this mean that all aspects of IPR are adequately covered by this legal framework? Some of the IPR related issues which are not provided under the legal framework include: (1) plant breeder's rights (PBR); (2) traditional biological knowledge; and (3) traditional copyright.

PBR laws provide protection for new plant varieties developed by breeders. Several countries have put in place laws that protect PBR. For example, in Australia, PBR is protected under the *Plant Breeder's Act* 1994. The registration of the right protects trees or vines up to 25 years and 20 years for these species.

Traditional biological knowledge is critical to biodiscovery and biotechnology. The use of traditional knowledge can expedite research progress and reduce costs in research and may lead to quick and effective results. Using traditional knowledge to develop new drugs and genetically modified organisms for commercialization is a growing industry. The protection given to the use and management of traditional knowledge is very scarce at the global level. PNG is one of those countries that do not have a law relating to the protection of traditional biological knowledge and the use and management of the same.

Traditional IPR is protecting 'tradition based' intellectual property which includes knowledge system, creations, innovations and cultural expressions. The integration of traditional IPR and traditional knowledge is a new process that has been introduced only recently into the IPR regime. Since the adoption of the CBD and the creation of WIPO, attempts have been made at the local level (domestic) to test this process particularly in the developing countries. In PNG, efforts were made through the *Copyright and*

Neighbouring Rights Act and *Patents and Industrial Designs Act* to promote this integration.

The discussions that follow will focus on the protection of traditional biological knowledge because of the important role that TK play in the development of new ideas that lead to the commercialization of biological resources. At this juncture it must be noted that no adequate protection has been provided in the present legal regime for the protection of plant breeders, particularly the traditional plant breeders.

The Legal Framework on IPR

There are several pieces of legislation which will be considered under this heading. These are: (1) *Patents and Industrial Designs Act* 2000; (2) the *Copyright and Neighbouring Rights Act* 2000; (3) *Trade Marks Act* 1978; (4) *National Agriculture Research Institute Act* 1996 and (5) the *Income Tax Act* 1958 (consolidated to No.68 of 2000). Each of these legislations and their specific provisions which impact on IPR and their relevance to ABS are considered below. The first two pieces of legislation were enacted in 2000 as a response to the demands by the World Trade Organization and World Intellectual Property Organization (WIPO) in the early 1990s. Both statutes were introduced in PNG under immense pressure from WIPO to enable the country to meet deadlines set by the organization. It was in 1997 that PNG became a member of WIPO. This was soon after its accession to TRIP.

Designs and Patents

The shapes or appearances of manufactured goods are referred to as designs. In PNG, the registration and protection of designs are covered by the *Patents and Industrial Designs Act 2000*. The legislation was enacted in 2000 for the purpose of providing a framework and the protection of industrial property rights namely; patents, industrial designs and geographical indications and for related purposes. The Act is the primary legislation dealing with one form of IPR – patents. Part I, like other statutes, deals with preliminary matters, Part II establishes the office of the registrar, his or her powers and functions and other administrative arrangements. Part III and IV deal with patents and industrial designs respectively. Part V deals with miscellaneous matters and part VI provides for subsequent promulgation of regulations to the Act.

The objective of the law is to control the visual appearance of manufactured products. Patents on the other hand, is related to new knowledge that leads to the improvements in products and processes. Patents are also protected under *Patents and Industrial Designs Act*. Generally there are two types of patent. The first is 'standard patent' which is the long term protection given to the inventor. Under the *Patents and Industrial Designs Act* it is 50 years.

The second is 'innovation patent' which has a relatively short term and inexpensive.

Patents are defined by the Act as "patent" means the title granted to protect an invention." The legislation defines invention as:

> An idea of an inventor which permits in practice the solution of a specific problem in the field of technology and may be, or may relate to, a product or a process, but does not include-
> (a) a discovery, scientific theory or mathematical method; or
> (b) a scheme, rule or method for—
> (i) doing business; or
> (ii) performing purely mental acts; or
> (iii) playing games; or
> (c) diagnostic, therapeutic and surgical methods, but not including any products for use in any such methods, for the treatment of humans or animals

According to this definition, the following things do not qualify as patents under the Act:

- A discovery
- Scientific theory
- Mathematical method
- Scheme, rule or method for doing business
- Scheme, rule or method for performing mental acts
- Scheme, rules or method for playing games
- Diagnostic method
- Therapeutic method
- Surgical method

The Act also defines industrial design. It states that:

> … "industrial design" means any composition of lines or colours or any three-dimensional form, or any material, whether or not associated with lines or colours, provided that such composition, form or material gives a special appearance to a product of industry or handicraft and can serve as a pattern for a product of industry or handicraft and appeals to and is judged by the eye

The thrust of the legislation is to protect patents and industrial designs from exploitation. The Act does this through the creation of the office of the Registrar of Patents and Industrial Designs under s4 and the creation of a Register of Patents and a Register of Industrial Designs. The Registrar's principal function under the Act is to register patents and industrial designs and ensure that they are protected from exploitation. The registration of a patent or industrial design under the Act entitles the owner to certain rights and protection under the legislation.

Under the legislation a person can apply for the registration of a patent under Part III (sections 12-37) and an industrial design under Part IV (sections 38-51) of the Act. According to s31, when a patent is registered it is valid for 20 years. Industrial designs on the other hand, when registered, are protected for only five years. However, according to s50 an industrial design can be renewed for a further two or five year period.

When a patent or industrial design is registered, the owner is required under the legislation to pay annual registration fees for its continued protection under the Act. The relevant fees are prescribed in the Schedule to the *Patents and Industrial Designs Regulation* 2002. The legislation also vests certain rights and privileges on the owners of patents and designs.

This legislation must be read together with the *Income Tax Act*. The tax legislation imposes taxes on income earned from revenue derived from the use of the patents and industrial designs. The taxation aspects of patents and industrial designs are dealt with under Chapter 8.

There are no specific provisions that cater for the protection of traditional biological knowledge. In fact traditional biological knowledge is explicitly excluded by the operation of Section 13(2) of the *Patents and Industrial Designs Act*. That section reads:

> For purpose of this section, prior art shall consist of everything disclosed to the public, anywhere in the world, by –
> a) tangible form; or
> b) oral disclosure; or
> c) use; or
> d) any other way,
> prior to the filing, or, where appropriate, the priority date of the application claiming the invention.

According to this provision, traditional biological knowledge would not pass the test of 'novelty' if is shown that it is anticipated by 'prior art'. The definition of 'prior art' would by operation make traditional biological knowledge unpatentable.

Biological inventions and processes would definitely be protected by this legislation. For example a researcher who invents a technology to extract fluid from *noni* to cure tuberculosis; the apparatus created for extraction is an invention. The inventor can seek protection under the Act. Any step by step method taken to acquire the vaccine is called the process, which is also protected under the Act. This is the biotechnology of the researcher (developer) that is being protected. Eventually the product or the vaccine would be produced and marketed to the public. Any designs that gives certain appearance and appealing to the eye is a pattern of the product. This is referred to as industrial design and is protected under the Act.

The real issue is whether the rights of holders of traditional biological knowledge who contribute to a biological invention which is registered under this legislation are recognized. An additional issue is whether the Act protects the rights of indigenous community and the custodians of the genetic resources from a particular locality. The legislation does not cover these two issues therefore holders of traditional biological knowledge are not protected under this legislation. The Act has been fashioned to protect industrial property rights and thus excludes traditional biological knowledge and genetic resources. An invention using traditional knowledge can therefore not be patented.

Copyright

IPR are currently protected under the *Copyright and Neighbouring Rights Act* 2000. The legislation was developed under the aegis of the World Intellectual Property Organization (WIPO) when PNG became a member of WIPO on 10th July, 1997. Being a member of WIPO, PNG had to ensure that the legislation was enacted before 2000 so that it could meet the deadline under the TRIPS Agreement. The *Copyright and Neighbouring Rights Act* is a standard WIPO law which has been adopted to suit PNG's circumstances. This legislation and the *Patents and Industrial Designs Act* must be considered together. The latter relates to industrial property rights while the *Copyrights and Neighbouring Rights Act* is primarily to protect intellectual property rights taking the form of works, performances, sound recordings and broadcasts.

Copyright is the protection of the original idea that is expressed, and not the actual idea. In PNG, the right is protected under the Act. Copyright is the most common form of protection of intellectual property. This protection covers original material in:

- Literary work and compilations (journals, novels, screenplays, poems, song lyrics, published editions and reports, anthologies, directories and database);
- Artistic works, (painting, drawings, cartoons, sculpture, craft work, photographs, maps and plans):
- Dramatic or musical works:
- Films, broadcasts, sound recordings, multimedia; and
- Computer programs and databases.

All these will qualify as copyright under the Act. The relevant provisions of the Act are considered below.

There are five parts to *Copyright and Neighbouring Rights Act*. Part I deals with definitions of terms and phrases. Part II and III deal with copyrights and neighbouring rights respectively. Part IV deals with enforcement. Part V provides a protection mechanism for 'expression of folklore'. Part VI which is the miscellaneous provisions deal with matters such as the scope of the application of international law and others.

The scope of protection provided by the legislation is stipulated under Section 3. Section 5 expands the scope of Section 3 by enumerating the types of work that are protected by the legislation. Protection of biological inventions is veiled in these two provisions. The type of biological invention that may be protected under this Act would include soft technology such as computer software, instructional manuals and published texts relating to a biological invention developed by Papua New Guineans and foreigners living and working in PNG. An imported soft technology relating to a biological invention may be protected under this legislation. The process of invention is however, excluded from protection by Section 5 of the Act.

The owner of copyright has protection over his or her work during his or her lifetime and 50 years after his or her death. This is a standard period of protection provided under the TRIPS. When compared to the *Patents and Industrial Designs Act*, the protection provided by this legislation is very weak. The legislation does not provide a mechanism for registering copyright and also for monitoring of the unscrupulous use of copyright.

The legislation uses the old phrase 'expression of folklore' instead of TK. Section 2 defines 'expression of folklore' as:

> a group-oriented and tradition-based creation of groups or individuals reflecting the expectations of the community as an adequate expression of its cultural and social identity, its standards and values as transmitted orally, by imitation or by other means, including:
> (a) folktales, folk poetry and folk riddles; and
> (b) folk songs and instrumental folk music; and
> (c) folk dances and folk plays; and
> (d) production of folk arts in particular drawings, paintings, carvings, sculptures, pottery, terra cotta, mosaic, woodwork, metalware, jewelry, handicrafts, costumes and indigenous textiles.

This definition is broad and covers any traditional knowledge. Further, Section 30 stipulates that:

> 1. Expressions of folklore are protected against:
>   (a) reproduction; and
>   (b) communication to the public by performance, broadcasting, distribution by cable or by other means; and

(c) adaptation, translation and other transformation when such uses are made either for commercial purposes or outside their traditional or customary context.

2. Subsection (1) shall not apply where acts referred to therein are related to:
   (a) the use by a person exclusively for his own personal purposes; and
   (b) using short excerpts for reporting current events to the extent justified by the purpose of providing current information; and
   (c) the use solely for the purposes of face-to-face teaching or for scientific research.
3. In all publications and in connection with any communication to the public of any identifiable expression of folklore, its source shall be indicated in an appropriate manner and in conformity with fair practice and by mentioning the community or place from where the expression utilized is derived.
4. The right to authorize acts referred to in Subsection (1) and the terms and conditions of such authorization shall vest in a competent authority as determined by the Minister for the purposes of this section.
5. All monies collected in relation to this Part shall be used for purposes of cultural development as the competent authority referred to in Subsection (4), on the approval of the Minister, determines.

Anyone who intends to reproduce, perform, broadcast, distribute, adopt, translate or transform expression of folklore will obtain authority from a competent authority. Section 30(4) establishes the competent authority. It is not specific on what constitutes a competent authority. However, it states that, that authority will be determined by the minister. The competent authority which collects the money will use the money for cultural development.

There is no legislative arrangement for any benefits derived to be used by the indigenous community. There is specific purpose for which the money collected ought to be used and that is for cultural development. Further, the Act defines 'derivative works' under Section 2 which links it particularly to Section 4(1)(b). Section 4(1) (b) states:

> derivative works including in particular:
> (i) translations, adaptations, arrangements and other transformations or modifications of works; and
> (ii) collections of works and databases, whether in machine, readable or other forms; and
> (iv) collections of expressions of folklore provided that such collections are original by reason of the selection or arrangement of their contents.

This is indeed a wholesome protection and promotes the preservation of traditional culture. The legislation is however weak because it permits anyone to use with impunity another cultural group's expression of folklore just by mere selection or arrangement of their content, allows expression of folklore to be mutilated and debased. Further, scheme of the legislation severely restricts the protection under s30 of the Act.

It is an offence under Section 31 of the Act for a person to obtain an expression of folklore without the consent of the competent authority. Interestingly, it is not the consent of the indigenous people who are the owners of folklore but the competent authority. The guilty person then is liable to the competent authority for damages, injunction and other remedies as the court may deem fit.

In relation to TK, the Act provides protection over any traditional knowledge. A developer can have access to TK with the authorization from the competent authority. The payment for the use of the TK is not made to the indigenous people but the competent authority. The monies collected are to be used specifically for cultural development. This means that monies collected may not be used for other purposes such as reward to local holders of the TK. Although, the Act provides a blanket protection over all TK, the benefits accruing to the local communities is very limited.

Thus, Act does not provide protection for traditional biological knowledge and its uses for biotechnology. However, the Act will apply where the biological inventions or processes take the form of soft technology. The issue with the legislation is that benefits that may be derived from biological resources associated with TK will not be equitably shared consequently, the Act does not promote the attainment of the goals of sustainable development under the CBD.

Trade Marks

Trade marks are words, symbols, pictures, sounds, smell or a combination of these. The registration of these marks distinguishes the goods and services of one trader from those of another. Trade marks are registered and protected under the *Trade Marks Act*.

The aim of this legislation is to protect trade marks. Trade marks is defined by Section 1 of the Act as:

> 'Trade mark' means a mark used or proposed to be used in relation to goods for the purpose of indicating, or so as to indicate, a connection in the course of trade between the goods and a person who has the right, either as proprietor or as registered user, to use the mark whether with or without an indication of the identity of that person

In so far as it relates to IPR, there is little the legislation does to protect those rights. However, this legislation will become significant when dealing with the commercialization of a biological invention.

When a raw biological resource is ultimately developed as a commercial product for either economic, industrial or health use, it is then marketed for consumption. The inventor, at this stage, would like to use a mark to market and sell the products of his labour. The *Trade Mark Act* becomes significant here to indicate a relationship between a person, who maybe a proprietor or a registered user and the products or goods which are being traded.

Institutional IPR

Several institutions in the country are developing regulatory frameworks relating to IPR issues. For instance the University of Papua New Guinea has developed a draft ABS policy which spells out the percentages of benefits distribution amongst the major stakeholders engaged in biological resources research and development, which is awaiting final approval by the University Council. The National Forest Institute is also said to have developed a similar policy.

The most explicit legal protection of institutional IPR is provided under the *National Agriculture Research Institute Act* 1996. The legislation which establishes the National Agriculture Research Institute states in unequivocal terms that the IPR and patents that emerge as a result of performing the institute's functions rests with the institute. The relevant provisions of the Act are Sections 40 and 43. Section 43 empowers the Institute to use research results obtained in the performance of its functions under this Act for commercial purposes through business activities with or through joint venture partnerships with any public or private body. The commercialization of plant genetic resource for food and agriculture (PGRFA) raises issues of ownership and benefit sharing. In this instance Section 40 of the Act expressly states that all 'intellectual properties and patents designed and derived from the work of the Institute are the sole property of the Institute, and the Institute shall have legal and sole right to protect these properties and patents and may take legal action against any person or organization violating this right.'

Section 40 therefore, vests the ownership of all biological inventions by NARI scientists in the institution. It would follow that only NARI as an institution can register patents under the *Patents and Industrial Designs Act*. Can NARI scientists be registered as co-owners of the patents? Unfortunately, Section 40 excludes them from gaining any interests in a patent.

Protection of Traditional Biological Knowledge

A review of the legal framework relating to patents, copyright and industrial designs show that it does not provide for the protection of traditional biological knowledge. This situation raises a series of critical issues including: (1) What is to be the area of disclosure or use of traditional knowledge? (2) Would the terms of an ABS include the disclosure and use of traditional knowledge within indigenous communities? (3) What happens if a developer tumbles upon traditional knowledge and patents the knowledge without knowing that the knowledge belongs to a indigenous community? The legal framework is not clear on these issues. These are issues that may have to be resolved by the new ABS framework.

Summary

International instruments clearly provide for ABS relating to biological resources and associated traditional knowledge. States are required to allow access to their biological resources and ensure that equitable sharing of benefits arising from the sustainable utilization of these resources accrues to all the relevant stakeholders. The general view of CBD is that if a product or process existed in a culture or community for a long period of time, it is owned and hence protected under intellectual property law. This conflicts with the TRIPS regime. Under TRIPS if IPR is not patented, it is not owned. If it is not owned it represents knowledge that is a common heritage of mankind and must be available for exploitation by those who wish to do so.

The regulatory framework on IPR in PNG is of no assistance to owners of genetic resources and traditional knowledge holders. The statutes on IPR reviewed do not cater for and protect holders of traditional biological knowledge and local communities. At the time of the enactment of the current IPR laws, ABS was never considered as an issue by the policy and law-makers. The existing pieces of legislation are sector or specific issue oriented. For example, the *Trade Mark Act* is a specific legislation on marks used by proprietors of goods or services to establish a connection with the proprietor and the goods or services. The other two laws; the *Copyright and Neighbouring Rights Act* and the *Patents and Industrial Designs Act* are specifically focused on expressed ideas and inventions respectively.

On the other hand *Income Tax Act* and *National Agriculture Research Institute Act* do not specifically provide for the protection of IPR. In the case of the *Income Tax Act* 1959 (as amended), it makes a provision for the taxation of benefits derived from IPR, whereas the latter establishes the ownership over intellectual properties and patent designs derived from the work of the National Agriculture and Research Institute. The term intellectual property is an open term. Does that cover PBR, biodiscovery and biotechnology, etc? These are issues that need to be addressed by the new ABS regime.

An issue that is of paramount importance is whether the existing laws adequately cater for IPR of individuals and persons operating under an ABS regime. In the case of the National Agriculture Research Institute, if any biodiscovery falls within the ambit of intellectual property under Section 40 of the Act, it will be protected by the legislation. The legislations namely, the *Patents and Industrial Designs Act*, and the *Trade Marks Act* protect the developer (that is; the researcher and the manufacturer). The only protection that the traditional knowledge holder has is under the *Copyright and Neighbouring Rights Act*. The Act provides a wide protection - however, there is no provision on fair and equitable sharing of benefits derived from these resources.

In these circumstances, the holders of TK and local communities will stand to gain a fair share of benefits from the sustainable use of their biological resources through Material Transfer Agreements. The MTA allows for greater flexibility which can be utilized by the resource owners and the other parties to sort out their differences and conclude amicable terms for all the stakeholders. Nonetheless, a national ABS framework can provide useful and stronger protection to all the relevant stakeholders engaged in an ABS related project. There is a need to establish a workable structure through an appropriate legal mechanism to expand the scope of the IPR to cover TK and protection to holders of TK.

Chapter 9. Access and Benefit Sharing: The Taxation Regime

Mark Opur

Introduction

Liability to taxation in PNG is premised on the basis that a taxpayer is a national of PNG, but if he is not a national then he is resident in PNG. If the taxpayer is not a national and he is not resident in PNG then he will be liable to PNG taxation if the source of his income is located in PNG. This short Chapter looks specifically at the tax treatment of benefits arising from the development of intellectual property such as patent, copyright, design or license and the nature of expenditure incurred in the production and or development of such property.

For discussion purposes certain assumptions are being made. The first assumption relates to persons who own a patent, copyright or design. They are assumed to be nationals of PNG or if not then they are resident in PNG. Secondly, the source of their income from the use or sale of a patent, copyright or a design will be deemed to have a source in PNG. Any receipt of payment (including royalty) from the sale, transfer, or licensing of a unit of property by the owner will be income in his hands. This certainly includes the transfer or assignment of a right to receive such payments to a third party.

This Chapter does not attempt to discuss what payments is not strictly income or details of whether a particular payment is income in the hands of the recipient. However it is made clear through out the discussion the distinction between a payment that is of a capital nature and that which has connotations of a payment of revenue nature. This distinction is necessary because a payment, which is capital in nature, is not subject to tax while all payments of a revenue nature are subject to taxation.

It also becomes necessary to have a look at the nature of expenditure incurred by the owner of a patent, a copyright or the design and development of such patent or copyright. The relief provided by the *Income Tax Act* (1959) (as Amended) to the owner is only available where expenditure is incurred in producing income that is subject to tax. In other words, the owner of a patent, copyright or a design can claim deduction on the expenditure incurred with the research, design and production of such patent or copyright if it results in producing assessable income.

The Legislative Scheme

Division 12 of the *Income Tax Act* specifically covers taxation on income from intellectual property or rights to income from intellectual property. While this Division covers deductions on expenditure, the general deduction provisions are also applicable. The thrust of the discussion in this Chapter is therefore solely centered on the relevant provisions of the *Income Tax Act.*

However, other relevant pieces of legislation such as the *Stamp Duties Act* and the *International Agreements Act* are also considered and their relevancy discussed very briefly. This basically relates to double taxation and how a certain income is allocated to a particular taxing jurisdiction to impose its taxation.

Definition

Division 12 of the *Income Tax Act* covers intellectual property and is inclusive of sections 171 to 185. Much of the discussion is centered on these provisions and is confined to the tax treatment of benefits arising from intellectual property rights. The provisions on assessablitiy of income and on deductions are each discussed separately.

The definition provisions in Section 171 refer to the word 'owner' and phrase 'unit of industrial property' and they are constantly referred to in subsequent provisions. The starting point therefore is to know what they mean.

The person who possesses rights in respect of a 'unit of industrial property' is the 'owner' A unit of industrial property is defined to mean rights possessed by a person who is the owner of patent granted in PNG, the owner of a copyright subsisting in PNG, the owner of a design registered in PNG, or the owner of a license under such patent, copyright or design. This definition is all encompassing and would almost certainly include the activities from early research (whether biological or otherwise) through to the finalization or completion and registration of a particular design, patent or copyright with the Intellectual Property Office of PNG.

The above definition extends to include equitable rights to a patent, copyright or design or in respect of a license under such a patent, copyright or design. Any amounts derived as consideration for an absolute or partial assignment of a patent, trademark, copyright and similar property will be income in the ordinary meaning of the word.

Royalty which is certainly income in the hands of the recipient is sometimes paid or credited as consideration for the use of, or the right to use, any copyright, patent, design or model, plan, secret formula or process, trademark or other like property or right.[63] The assessable income of a taxpayer will include any such payments made under different scenarios mentioned above.[64] This means a payment that is made to the owner of a property (whether patent or copyright or any such property) is assessable whether this is of an income or capital nature provided it is paid as or by way of a royalty. Such royalty payments will be treated as income from property where it is paid in respect of a patent, license or other rights to use the property. It is generally accepted that the source of royalty payments in consideration of industrial property rights is where the rights are registered or located, and the source of payments for use or supply of technological information (which is protectable) will most likely be the place where the contract is made or where the information is handed over. If any development of a particular design, patent or copyright takes place in PNG and is registered with the Intellectual Property Office of PNG, the source of payments made as royalty will certainly be PNG and subject to PNG tax.

Application

Division 12 applies in the following situations to an owner of a unit who has used it for the purpose of producing assessable income. Firstly, where the owner incurred capital expenditure in development, devising the invention in respect of which a patent is granted, producing the work in which copyright first subsists or producing the design and obtaining its registration. Secondly, it applies to a situation where the owner incurred capital expenditure on the purchase of the unit of industrial property. Thirdly, the Division applies to a scenario where the owner acquired the unit for no valuable consideration from an owner who had been allowed or was entitled to deduction under this Division.[65]

The above three scenarios are the only situations which must exist for Division 12 to apply. If none of these is present, then Division 12 is not applicable, and therefore, cannot be applied.

Deductions

It is the 'owner' of a 'unit of industrial property' who, to qualify for deduction must either use it for the purpose of producing assessable income in the year of income, or having so used or having so used it in a prior year of income.[66] It is not necessary that the use by the owner of a unit of industrial property actually generates assessable income in order to meet the test of being "used …for the purpose of producing assessable income." The

63 . Refer to definition of "royalty" in section 4(1) of the *Income Tax Ac t*
64 . See section 47(1)(f)
65 . See section 172(1)(a, b & c)
66 . See section 172 (1)(d & e)

test would be satisfied once the unit is complete as a 'unit of industrial property' and that the unit is put to use with the object of ultimately producing assessable income.

A deduction is available to a taxpayer who was at the time during the year of income the owner of a unit of industrial property to whom Division 12 applies.[67] A deduction is calculated by dividing the residual value of the unit at the end of the year of income by the number of years in the effective life of the unit at the commencement of the year of income.[68] The minimum deduction is K100.00.[69] If the ownership lapses or the unit ceases to exist, a deduction is not allowable in the year of cessation.

Further, specific expenditure incurred (whether by payment of fees or otherwise) in the year of income in obtaining, or seeking to obtain a patent for an invention, registration of a design or a copyright or for any extension of a term or period is an allowable deduction.[70] A taxpayer can claim deduction on all such expenditures when he lodges his income tax return for that particular year of income.

Residual Value

The residual value is essentially ascertained by taking the *cost* of the unit *less* all *deductions* allowed or allowable under Division 12 to the owner for prior years and *consideration receivable* for any prior part disposal.[71]

The grant of a license is a part disposal.[72] Where a person who has been granted a licence surrenders that licence, he will not be deemed to have disposed off the unit unless the surrender was made in consideration for the payment to him of a lump sum and the person to whom the surrender has been made will not be deemed to have acquired a unit of industrial property by reason of the surrender only.[73] Surrender alone is not sufficient to dispose off a unit of industrial property. The person to whom a unit has been surrendered does not simply acquire the unit by virtue of the surrender. Any

---

67 . See section 173
68 . See section 173(1)
69 . See section 173(2)
70 . See section 91
71 . See section 178(1)
72 . See section 181(1)
73 . See sub(2) of s 181

extension of the term of the licence will be deemed to be the grant of a new licence.[74]

Effective Life

There are three categories of effective life, each measured from the commencement of the year in which the unit was first used, and extending to an end of year. Firstly, if the unit is acquired for a specified period, the earlier of the end of year in which the unit terminates or the specified period terminates. Secondly, if the unit relates to a patent or design or, at the end of the year of income during which the paten or design will terminate.[75] Thirdly, if the unit relates to a copyright, either the end of the year of income in which the copyright terminates, or the end of the year after 25 years from the date of ownership whichever is the earlier.

A patent is deemed to terminate at the expiration of 16 years after the date of the patent and a copyright is deemed to terminate on a date it ceases to subsist. A design is deemed to terminate 15 years after registration takes effect.[76]

A patent which is acquired after its term is extended is deemed to terminate at the end of the extension. A copyright originating from joint authorship extends for a period of 50 years after the death of the first author, or until the death of the second author, whichever is the later. Where the second author survives for more than 50 years after the death of the first author and the copyright is acquired during the extended period, the copyright is deemed to terminate on such a date as the Commissioner General determines having regard to the life expectancy of the surviving author.[77]

Amounts to be included in the Assessable Income

Section 175 makes provision for amounts received on disposal of a unit of industrial property to be included in the assessable income. Where a unit has been disposed off whether in part or wholly and the effective life of the unit has not expired, and consideration received exceeds the residual value of the unit, it is the amount in excess that must be included in the assessable income of the year of income.[78] In cases where the effective life of the unit has expired, the amount to be included in the assessable income is the amount of consideration receivable in respect of the disposal.[79]

---

[74]. See section 181(3)
[75]. See section 180(1)(a & b)
[76]. See section 180(2)©
[77]. See section 180(4)
[78]. See section 175(1)
[79]. See section 175(2)

The maximum amount to be included in the assessable income of a taxpayer in respect of a disposal of a unit of industrial property is not to exceed the total of deductions allowed or allowable. This of course excludes any assessable income of previous years to the taxpayer in respect of the same unit.

Cost

As previously mentioned in the discussion on residual value, the determination of residual value begins with determining the cost of the unit of industrial property. The cost will be the amount of capital expenditure incurred[80] or in the case of acquisition for no consideration, the residual value immediately before the disposal.[81]

Where capital expenditure has been incurred and the Commissioner General is of the opinion that it is excessive or if the unit was purchased together with other assets and no price is allocated to that unit, the cost of the unit will be that amount which is determined by the Commissioner General.[82] It is therefore possible that all units of industrial property will always have a cost.

Consideration Receivable

The consideration receivable on disposal of a unit will obviously be the sale price less any expenses incurred in the sale. This will be the amount that will be included in the assessable income for the year. Where the unit is sold together with other assets and it is not possible to allocate a separate amount to the unit, it will be that amount as determined by the Commissioner General.

If a unit is disposed off wholly, the consideration receivable will be an amount equal to the residual value. However, if it is partly sold, the consideration will be such amount as is determined by the Commissioner General.

It must be noted that the Commissioner General has a wide discretion to determine what cost is to be allocated to a particular unit of industrial property. This wide discretion also extends to determining what amounts are receivable on the disposal of a unit. This is important because it denotes how much tax is payable on disposal of a particular unit. If the Commissioner General determines that a higher amount is receivable then a high amount will be payable in taxes.

---

80 . This will include costs for an invention and being granted a patent for an invention, a copyright or costs associated with authoring a design and registration of such a design.

81 . See section 177(1)(b)

82 . See section 172(2)

Partnership Disposal

Sometimes a unit of industrial property is owned by two or more partners. Any one of the partners may decide to have their share of the ownership disposed off. In such situations there are separate taxing provisions governing the disposal.

If a partnership is dissolved and there is a change in the ownership of a unit of industrial property, the provisions of Division 12 will apply as if the persons who owned the unit before the change occurred, disposed off the units in whole to the persons who own the units after the change.[83] The consideration paid or payable will be equal to an amount that is agreed to be paid. The Commissioner General will again apply his discretion if no amount is specified and determine an amount to the consideration.

Use of Patent by the State

It is possible that a person who has a patent over a particular invention can sell it to the State for its use for a certain consideration. The owner of the patent will be deemed to have disposed of the patent in part, in consideration for the payment of a lump-sum by the State. The owner will not be subject to tax on income derived from part that has been disposed off.

It must be noted that a particular patent that falls within the ambit of this particular provision is not disposed of wholly. Even if it is, for taxation purposes it will be considered to be a pat disposal only.

Benefits arising from Overseas Rights

Section 185 relates to units of industrial property developed and used overseas. Since any such unit will be used in PNG, the Commissioner General may decide that any deduction allowable under Division 12 may be reduced by any such amounts he thinks fit having regard to its benefits. Both individuals and corporations and the State may use units of industrial property developed overseas.[84] This usually entails the payment of certain consideration and such payments will be included in the assessable income.

Stamp Duty

There is no separate stamp duty on disposal or sale of a unit of industrial property, whether it is a patent, copyright, design or grant of a license. If a unit of industrial property is sold together with other assets such as building or land, it will attract a stamp duty of five percent

---

[83] . See section 182

[84] . This may be done subject to the provisions of section 185

Double Tax Agreements

The basic reason for countries to have double taxation agreements is to avoid situations where a particular individual or company is taxed twice on the same income by two different taxing jurisdictions. A double tax agreement therefore aims to allocate taxing rights to different taxing jurisdictions (usually between two countries) to prevent double taxation on the same income.

PNG has entered into Double Taxation Agreements with several countries. All such agreements are included in the schedules of the *Income Tax (International Agreements) Act 1987*. There may be disagreements on taxing of royalties from units of industrial property between PNG and a treaty partner so one has to look at the relevant provisions in the relevant agreement to determine which country has the right to tax.

PNG has so far entered into double taxation agreements with Germany, United Kingdom, Canada, Australia, Korea, Fiji, Singapore, Malaysia. Negotiations with Indonesia and Thailand have already been finalized.

Summary

Division 12 of the *Income Tax Act* effectively covers all aspects of taxation on intellectual property. It specifically sets out what amounts are to be included in the assessable income of the owner of a unit of industrial property when such a unit is sold. This includes any amounts received from the licensing and assignment of a right to receive income from such units. It also gives the Commissioner General wide discretionary powers to determine the value of consideration receivable on disposal of a unit where there is no agreed figure.

Division 12 also provides relief to owners of units of industrial property and to other taxpayers who may subsequently become the owners. The relief is in the form of tax deductions on expenditures or costs incurred with the invention, development and or designing of a particular unit of industrial property. The application of s91 is also a relevant consideration.

Other relevant legislation on taxation of units of industrial property must be considered. The applicability of these legislations will depend on the nature of particular transactions regarding intellectual property rights.

BIBLIOGRAPHY

Cabrera Jorge, Greene George, and Rotherham Tom, ABS Management Tool Project: Summary Project Description, international expert workshop on access to genetic resources and benefit sharing.

Campbell, B., Clarke, J., Lucket, M., Matose, F., Musvoto, C. and I. Scoones. (1995) *Local-Level Economic Valuation of Savanna Woodland Resources: Village Cases From Zimbabwe*. International Institute for Environment and Development, London.

Dalal-Clayton, B. and Bass, S., (2002) *Sustainable Development Strategies: A Resource Book. Organisation for Economic Co-operation*, UNDP, New York.

Dargavel, J.B. (1978). "A Model for Planning the Development of Industrial Plantation," *Australian Forestry*, 4(2): 95-107.

Dolley, B., (2003) "Ensuring Grassroots Participation in Development Planning and Implementation", (Unpublished).

Easton, D., (1953) *The Political System,* Knopf, New York.

Filer, C. (ed) (1999) *Dilemmas of Development: the social and economic impact of the Porgera Gold Mine, 1989-1994*, NRI & ANU, Port Moresby.

Filer, C. with Sekhran, N. (1998) *Loggers, donors and resource owners. Policy that works for forests and people* (series no. 2), NRI & IIED, Port Moresby.

Glowka, L., Pisupati, B. and de Silva, S., (2001) *Access to Genetic Resources and Traditional Knowledge: Lessons from South and Southeat Asia. Proceedings of the South and Southeast Asia Regional Workshop on Access to Genetic Resources and Traditional Knowledge*, IUCN – The World Conservation Union.

Hague, R and Harrop, M., (1987) *Comparative Government and Politics: An Introduction,* Macmillan Education Ltd, Houndmills.

Ham, C and Hill, M., (1985) *The Policy Process in the Modern Capitalist State,* Wheatsheaf Books Ltd, Sussex.

Henne, G., Liebeg, K., Drews, A. and Plan, T., (2003) *Access and Benefit Sharing (ABS): An Instrument for Poverty Alleviation, Proposals for An International Regime*, German Development Institute, Bonn.

Heywood, A., (1997) *Politics,* Macmillan Press Ltd, Houndmills.

Holzkecht Hartmut, Policy Reform, Customary tenure and Stakeholder Clashes in Papua New Guinea's Rainforests, Customary Tenure Seminar, Paper No. 1.

Holling, C.S., Jines, D.D. and W.C. Clark. (1977). "Ecological Policy Design: A Case Study of Forest and Pest Management," in Norton, G.A. and C.S. Holling. (eds.). *Proceedings of a Conference on Forest Management, CP-77-6*. International Institute for Applied Systems Analyses, Luxemburg, Austria.

Hotelling, Harold. (1931). "The Economics of Exhaustible Resources," *Journal of Political Economics*, 32(2): 137 – 75.

Imbun, B. Y. and McGavin, P. A., (ed) (2001) *Mining in Papua New Guinea: Analysis & Policy Implications*, UPNG Press, Port Moresby.

Ingestad, T., Aronsson, A. and G.I. Agren. (1981). "Nutrient Flux Density Model of Mineral Nutrition in Conifer Ecosystems," *Studia Forestalia Suecia*, 160: 61-71.

Jackson, R., Peterson, R. and Stanley, O., (1995) "Final Report Towards Sustainable Development in the OK Tedi Impact Area", James Cook University, Townsville.

Janssen, Ron. and Jose E. Padilla. (1996). The Valuation and Evaluation of Management Alternatives for the Pagbilao Mangrove Forest. Collaborative Research in Economics of Environment and Development (CREED), London and Amsterdam. CREED Working Paper Series No. 9.

Jock Langford, Benefit Sharing, international expert workshop on access to genetic resources and benefit sharing.

Kalinoe K L., (1998) *Water Law and Customary Water Rights in Papua New Guinea*, UBSPD, New Delhi.

King, P, Lee, W and Warakai. (ed) (1985) *From Rhetoric to Reality? Papers from the Fifteenth Waigani Seminar,* University of Papua New Guinea Press, Port Moresby.

Kwa E., (2001) *Natural Resources Law of Papua New Guinea*, Law Book Co, Sydney.

Kwa E., (2004) *Biodiversity Law and Policy of Papua New Guinea*, Papua New Guinea Institute of Biodiversity, Port Moresby.

Kwa, E.P.H., (2001) "An Ecologically Sustainable Model of People Development: Three Propositions for Papua New Guinea" (Unpublished).

Kimmins, J.P. and K.A. Schoullar. (1982). "FORCYTE-11: A User's manual for the Eleventh Version of the FORest Nutrient Cycling and Yield Trend Evaluator." Canadian Forestry Service, Ottawa, Canada. (A Contract Report.)

Lindblom, C.E., 'Still Muddling, Not Yet Through', *Public Administration Review,* 39, 1979.

Mawuli, A. and Sanida, O., (2000) Landowners' Mineral Rent-Quest and Use in Papua New Guinea. Discussion Paper No.95. NRI, Port Moresby.

Pearse, P. H. (1990). *Introduction to Forestry Economics*. University of British Columbia Press, Vancouver.

Peigi Wilson, Indigenous and Local Communities: Community level Prior Informed Consent for Accessing Knowledge and genetic Resources, international expert workshop on access to genetic resources and benefit sharing.

Presscott, J., Gauthier, B. and Sodi, J.N.M., (2000) *Guide to Developing a Biodiversity Strategy from a Sustainable Development Perspective*, UNEP, UNDP, institute de l'energie et de l'environment de la Francophonie and Ministere de l'Environnement du, Quebec.

Salant, Stephen W. (1995). "The Economics of Natural Resource Extraction: A Primer for Development Economists," *The World Bank Research Observer*, 10(1): 93-111.

Smith, Adam. (1776). *An Inquiry into the Nature and Causes of the Wealth of Nations*.

Tom'tavala Y, "Yam Gardens in the Sea: The Marine Claims of the Trobriand Islanders of Papua New Guinea" (2000) 27 *Melanesian Law Journal* 77 at 95.

Turner, B.S., Bednarz, R.W. and J.B. Dargavel. (1977). "A Model to Generate Stand Strategies for Intensively Managed Radiata Pine Plantations," *Australian Forestry*, 40(4): 255-67.

Wildavsky, A., *Speaking Truth to Power: The Art and Craft of Policy Analysis*, Little Brown, Boston, 1979.

Government Documents:

Papua New Guinea Government; (2002) The Medium Term Development Strategy 2003-2007.

Papua New Guinea Government; (2004) The Medium Term Development Strategy 2005-2010.

PNG Department of Mining., (2003) "Sustainable Development Policy and Sustainability Planning Framework for the Mining Sector in Papua New Guinea" (Green Paper).

www.ingramcontent.com/pod-product-compliance
Lightning Source LLC
Jackson TN
JSHW050749140926
108091JS00021B/20